PIANO • VOCAL • GUITAR

THE VERY BEST OF  IDOLIZE YOURSELF

T0081992

ISBN 978-1-4584-0298-1

7777 W. BLUEMOUND RD. P.O. BOX 13819 MILWAUKEE, WI 53213

Visit Hal Leonard Online at
www.halleonard.com

DANCING WITH MYSELF

Words and Music by BILLY IDOL
and TONY JAMES

Very fast Rock

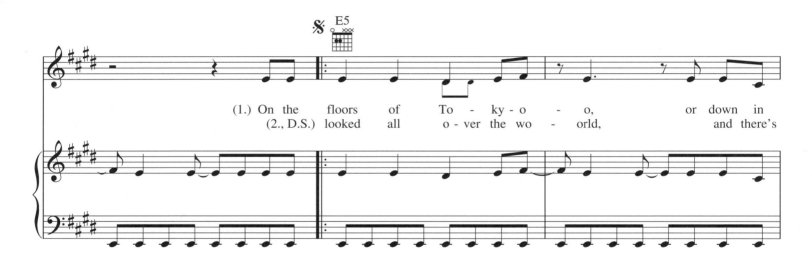

(1.) On the floors of To - ky - o - o, or down in
(2., D.S.) looked all o - ver the wo - orld, and there's

Lon - don town to go - go, oh, with the rec - ord se - lec - tion and the
ev - 'ry type of gi - irl. But,___ your emp - ty eyes___ seem to___

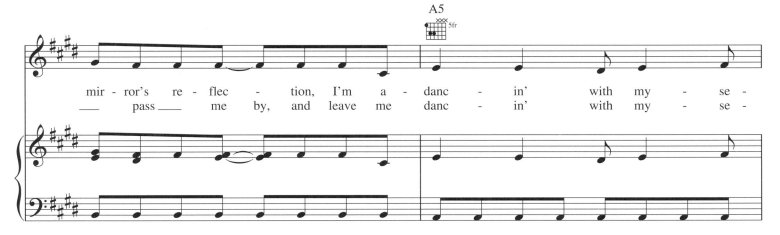

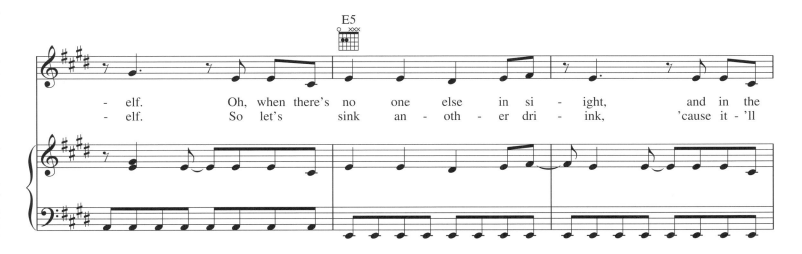

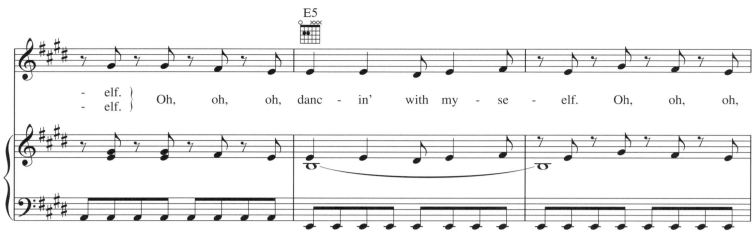

-elf. }
-elf. } Oh, oh, oh, danc - in' with my - se - elf. Oh, oh, oh,

danc - in' with my - se - elf. Well, there's noth - in' to lose, _____ and there's

noth - in' to prove, __ when I'm danc - in' with my - se -

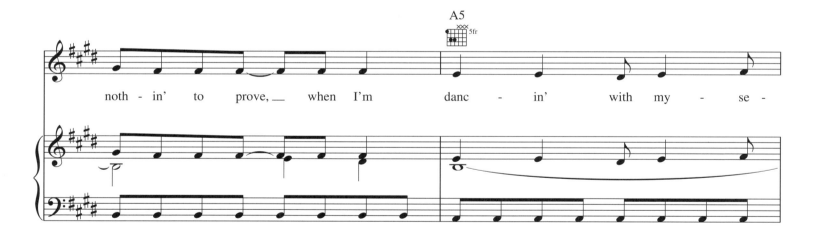

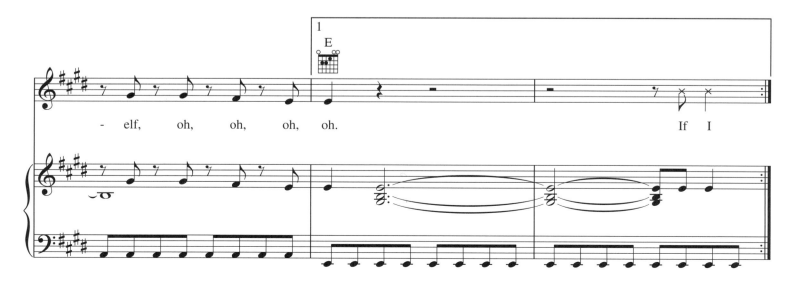

-elf, oh, oh, oh, oh.   If I

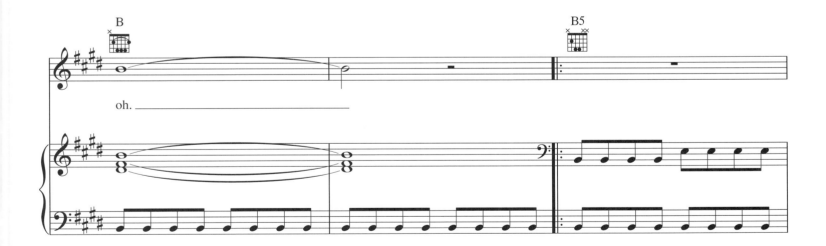

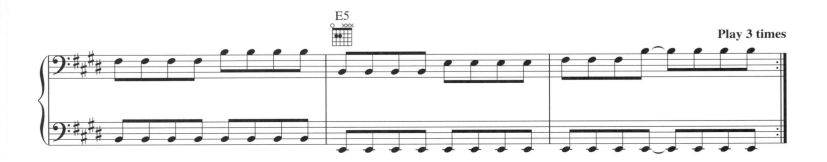

D.S. al Coda

CODA

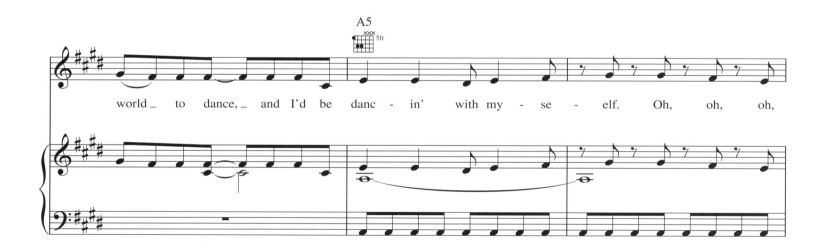

Well, _____ if I   had ___ the chance, _ I'd ask the

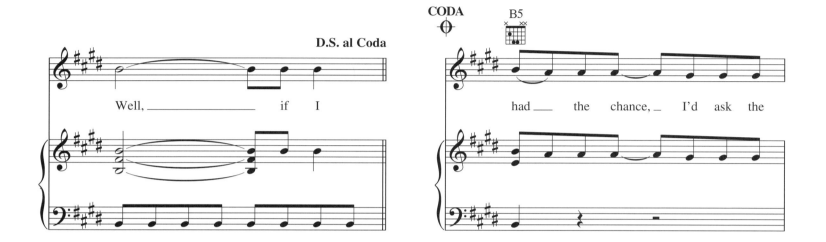

world _ to dance, _ and I'd be danc - in' with my - se - elf. Oh, oh, oh,

danc - in' with my - se - elf. Oh, oh, oh, danc - in' with my - se -

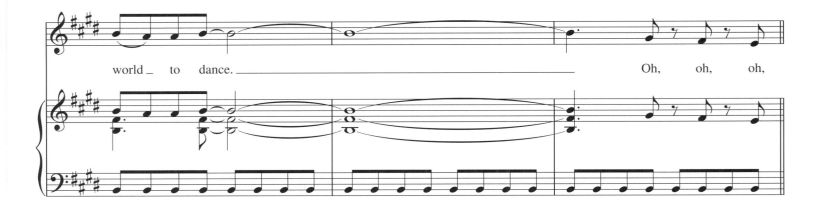

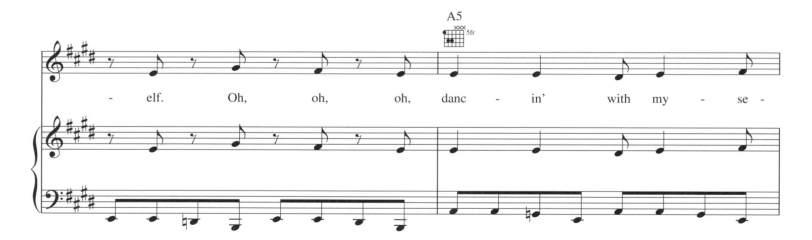

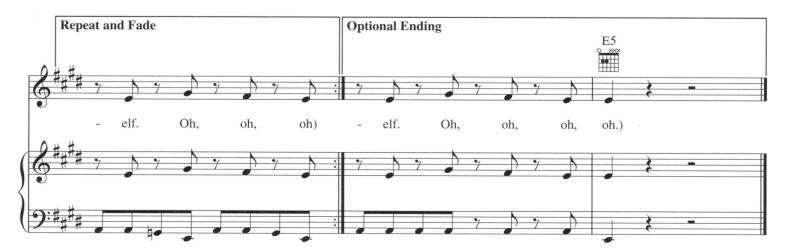

HOT IN THE CITY

Words and Music by
BILLY IDOL

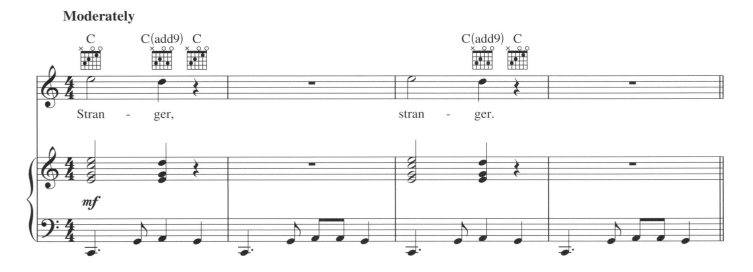

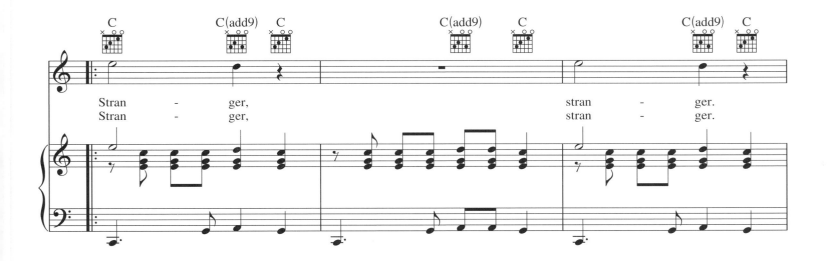

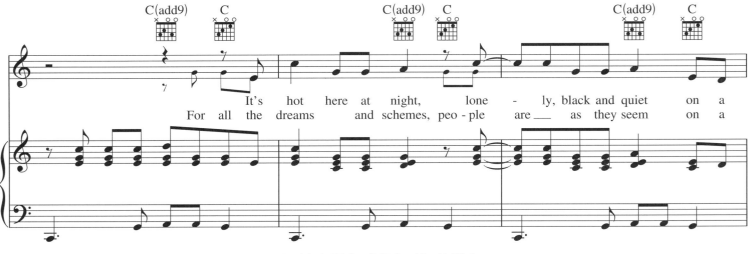

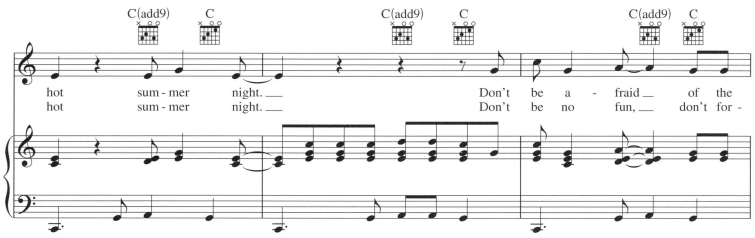

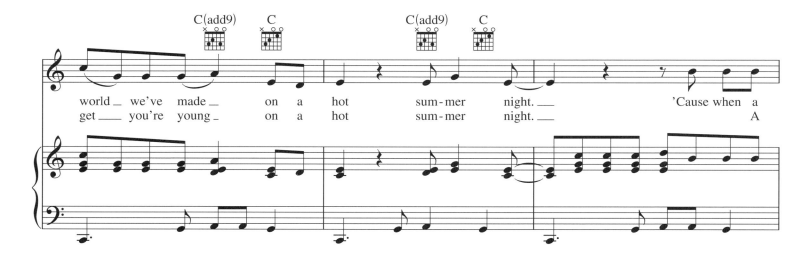

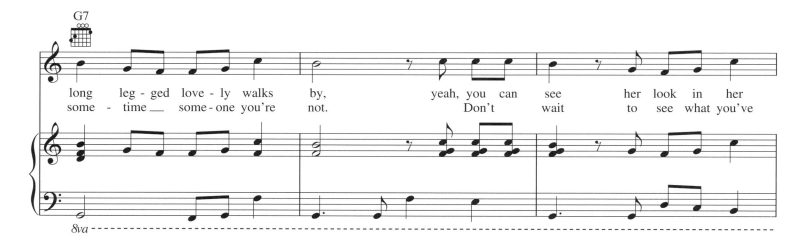

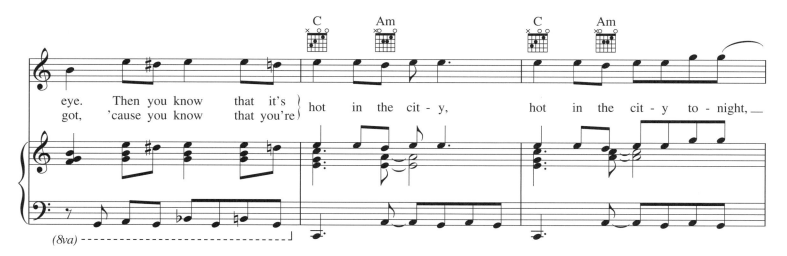

(1.,2.) (to - night.) ____   2. al - right.

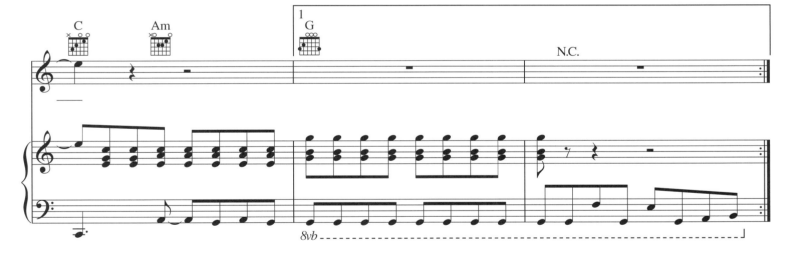

Hot in the cit - y, hot in the cit - y to - night, ____ (to - night.) __

And I'll move __ with the beat now. _____ I'm a train __ __ when I'm hate - ful _____ and I real -

- ly feel the heat now. _____ New York! __ Hot in the cit - y,

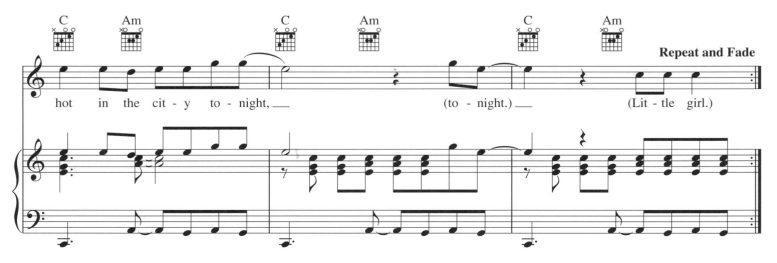

Repeat and Fade

hot in the cit - y to - night, ___ (to - night.) __ (Lit - tle girl.)

WHITE WEDDING

Words and Music by
BILLY IDOL

Fast Rock

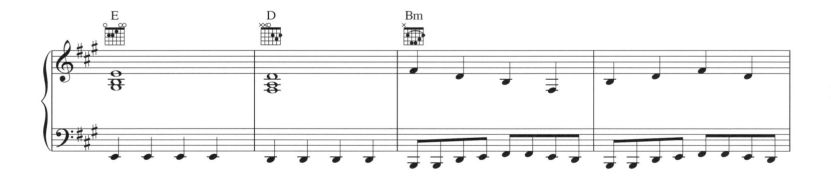

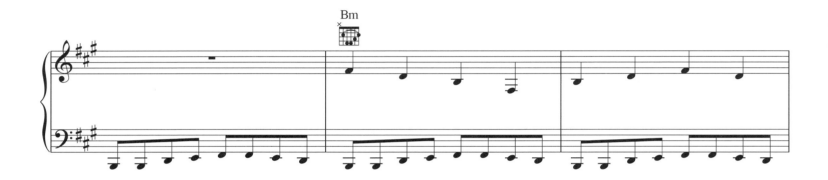

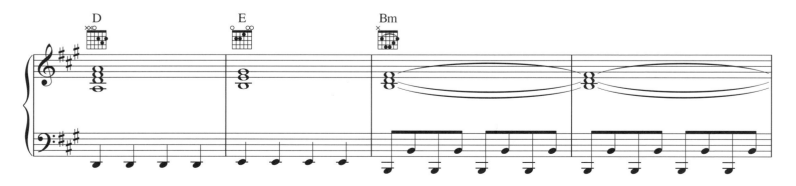

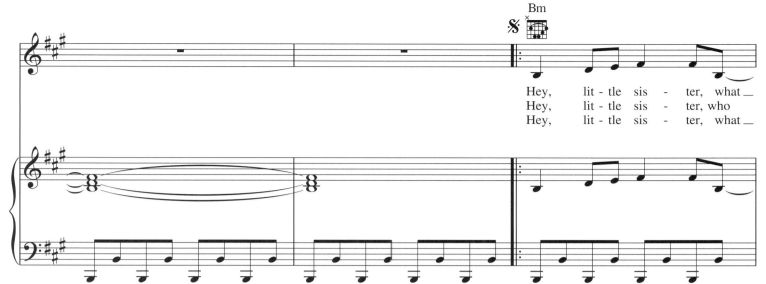

Hey, lit - tle sis - ter, what __
Hey, lit - tle sis - ter, who
Hey, lit - tle sis - ter, what __

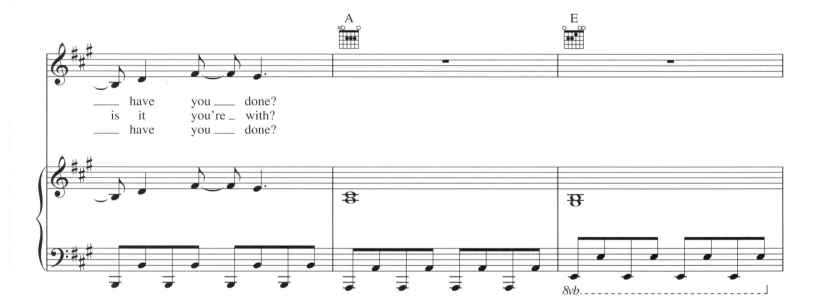

__ have you __ done?
is it you're _ with?
__ have you __ done?

Hey, lit - tle sis - ter, who's __ the on - ly one?
Hey, lit - tle sis - ter, what's __ your fas - ci - na - tion?
Hey, lit - tle sis - ter, who's __ the on - ly one?

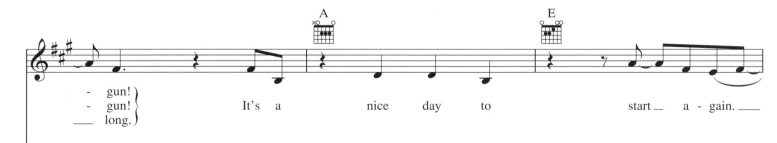

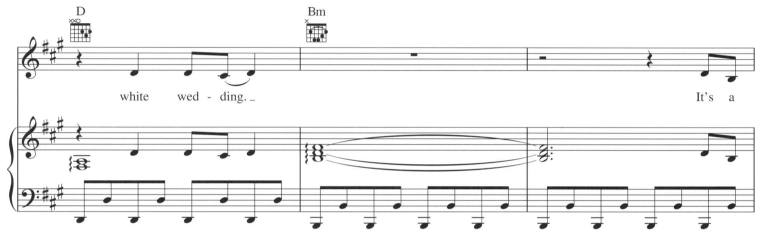

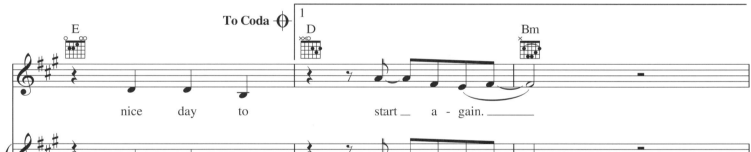

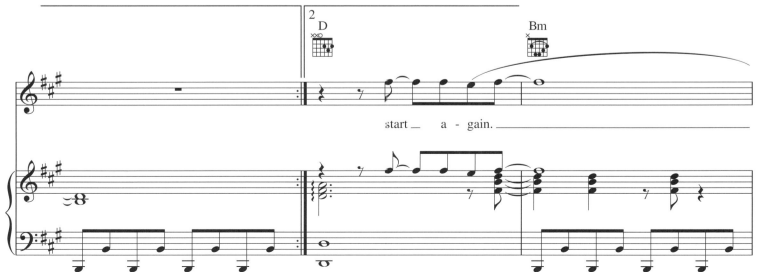

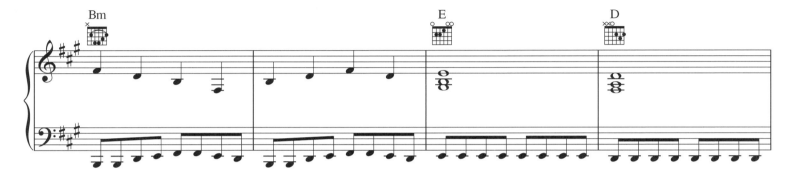

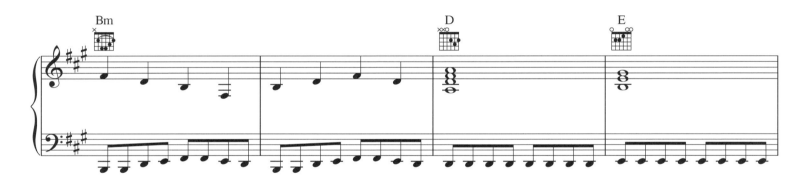

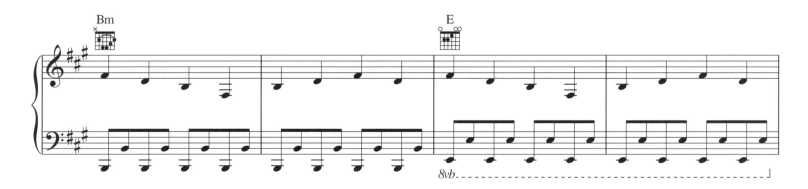

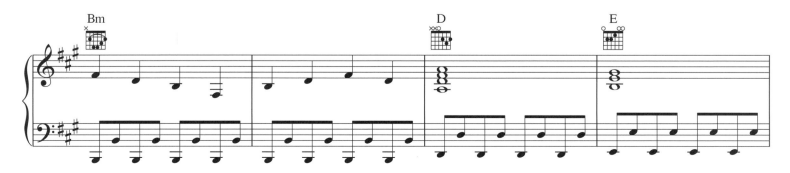

(Spoken:) Pick it up!

Take ___

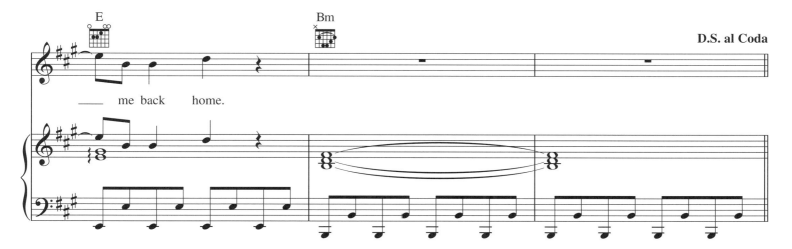

D.S. al Coda

___ me back home.

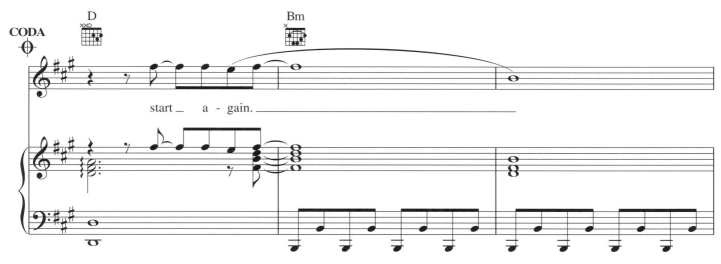

CODA

start ___ a - gain. ___

There is noth - ing left ___ in this

REBEL YELL

Words and Music by BILLY IDOL
and STEVE STEVENS

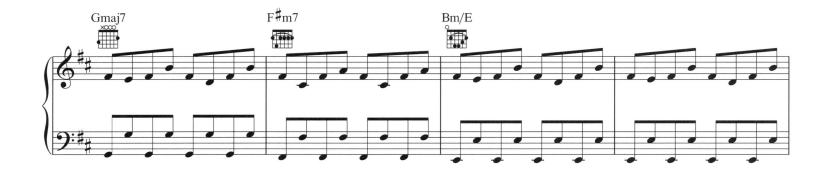

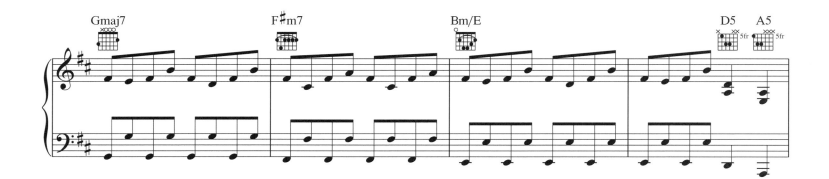

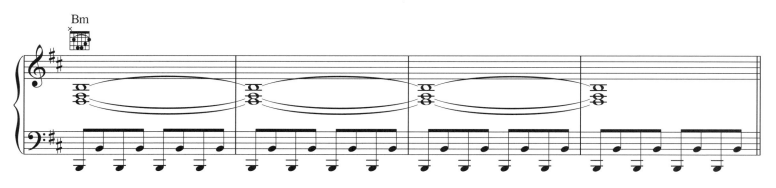

Last night _ a lit - tle danc - er   came danc - ing to my door. _
She don't _____ like _ slav - er - y,   she won't   sit and   beg.

Last night _ a lit - tle an - gel   came
But _ when _ I'm tired and lone - ly,   she

pump - ing on the floor. _   She said, _ "A - come, _
sees me to bed. ____   What _ set you _____

ba - by,   got a li - cense for _ love,
free and   brought you to me, babe?

In the mid-night hour, ___ babe, more, more, more, ___

___ with a re-bel yell, ___

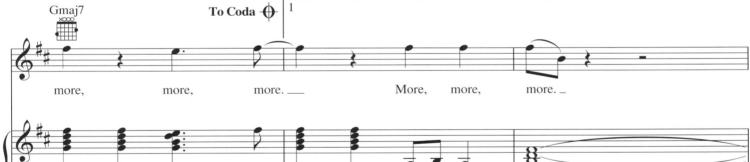

more, more, more. ___ More, more, more. _

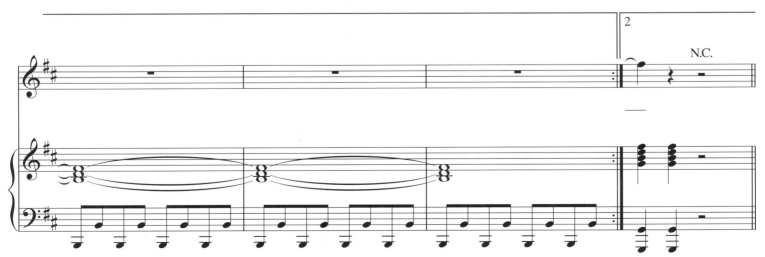

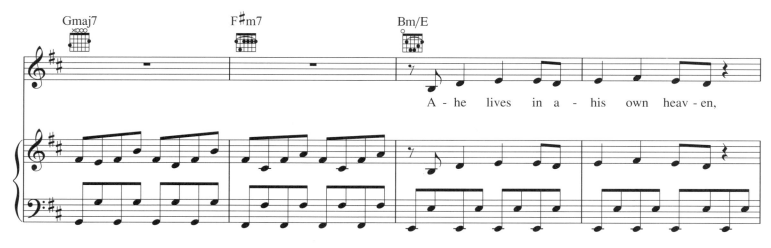

A - he lives in a - his own heav - en,

col - lects it to go from the

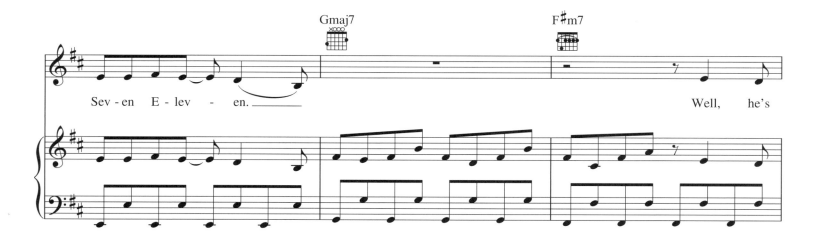

Sev - en E - lev - en. _____ Well, he's

out all night to col - lect a fare, _____

just so long, just so long it don't mess up his hair. _____

Guitar solo

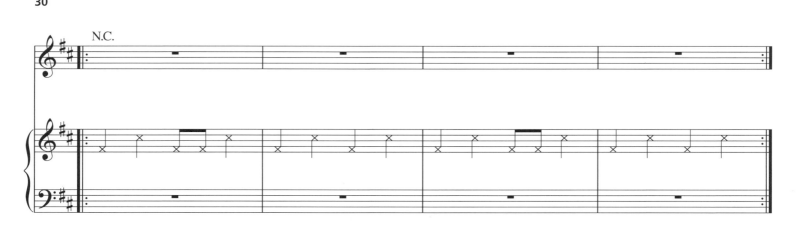

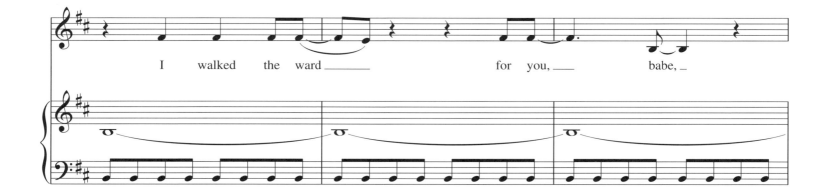

I walked the ward _____ for you, ___ babe, _

a thou - sand miles _ for you. _

I dried your

tears of pain,

a mil - lion times for you. ___

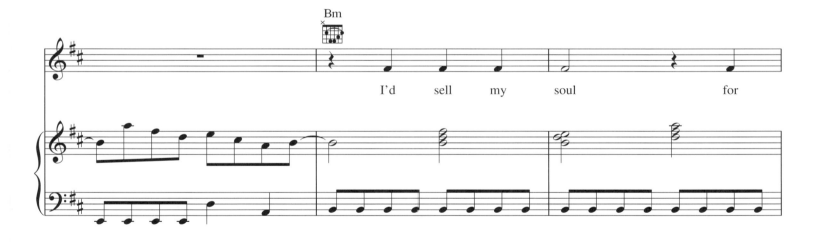

Bm

I'd sell my soul for

Bm/A

you, babe, ___ for mon - ey to burn ___

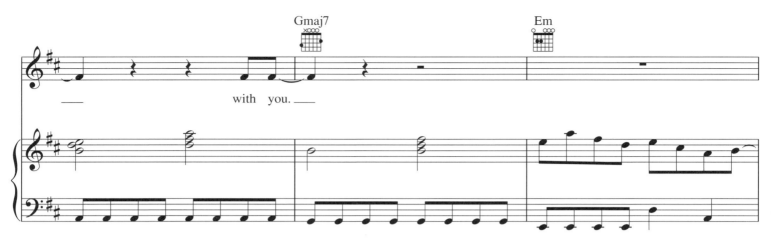

with you.

I give you all ____ and have none, babe, _

just - a, just - a, just - a, a - just - a to have you

here by me. Be - cause

D.S. al Coda

CODA

More, more,

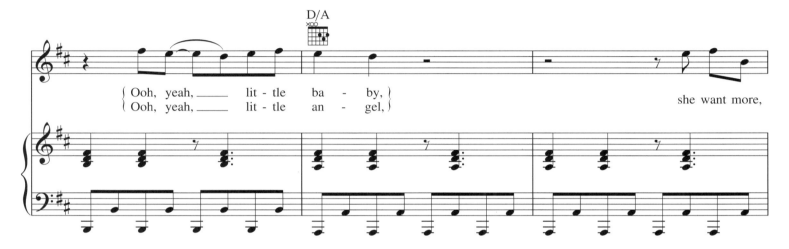

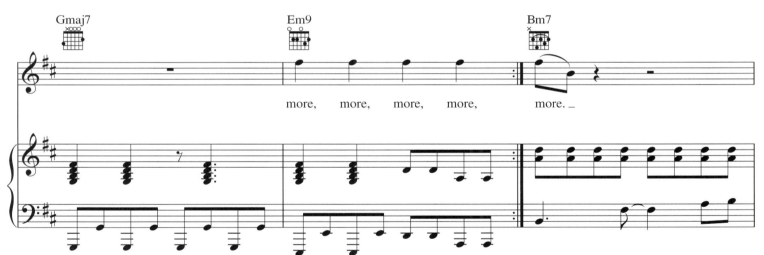

EYES WITHOUT A FACE

Words and Music by BILLY IDOL
and STEVE STEVENS

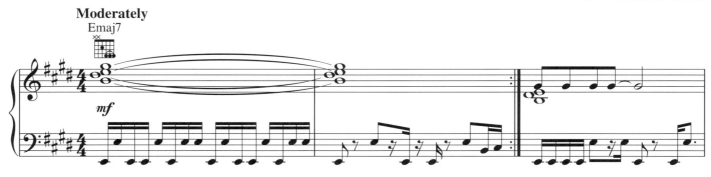

I'm all out of hope. ___ One more bad ___ dream ___

___ could bring ___ a fall. ___

When   I'm   far from __ home, __   don't call   me   on   the phone __
I   spend   so   much __ time __   be - liev - ing all   the   lies __

__   to tell   me you're __ a - lone. __   It's
__   to keep   the dream __ a - live. __

eas - y   to de - ceive; __   it's   eas - y   to tease __
Now   it   makes   me __ sad; __   it   makes   me   mad   at   truth __

but   hard   to   get   re - lease. __
for   lov - ing   what   was   you. __

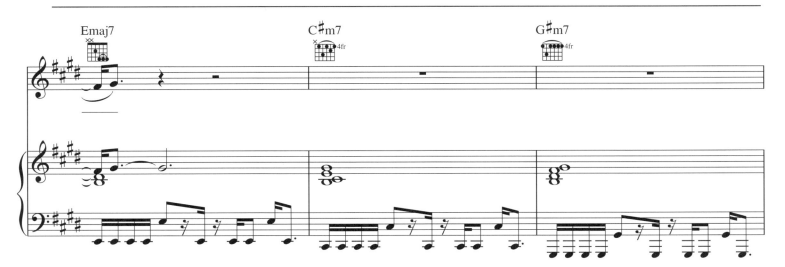

you're eyes ___ with-out ___ a face. ___

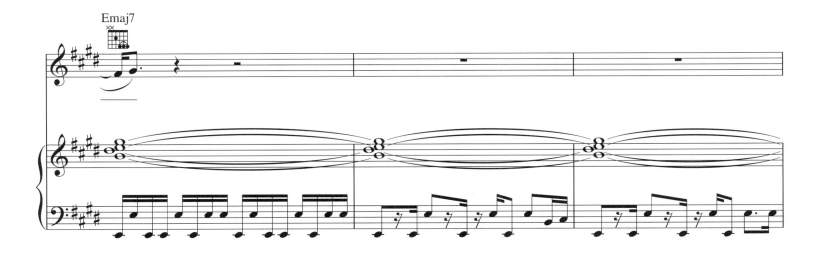

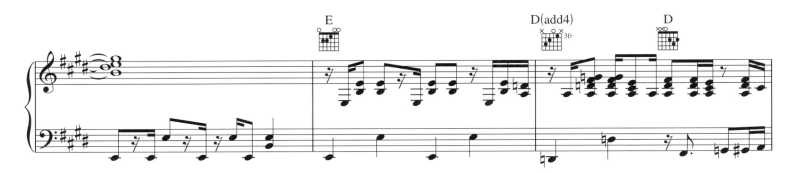

When
you hear the mu - sic, you __ make a dip in - to some-one else-'s pock-et, then __ make a slip. __

You steal a car and go __ to Las Ve - gas, __ ooh, gig - o - lo pool.

Hang - in' out by __ the state line, turn-ing ho - ly wa - ter in - to wine, __

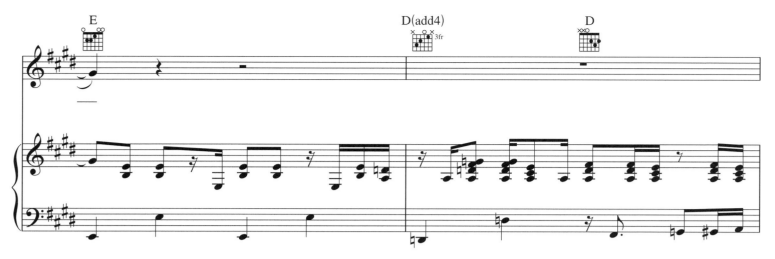

Now I close my eyes ___ and I won-der why ___

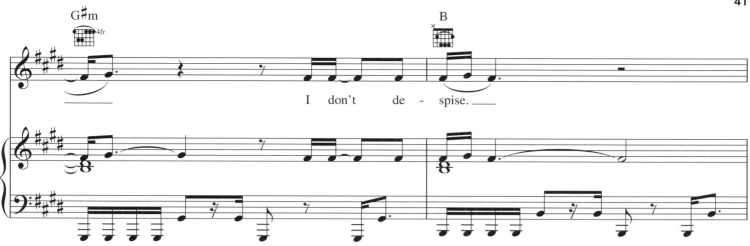

I don't de - spise.

Now all I can do. love what was once

so a - live and new. But it's gone from your

eyes, I'd bet - ter re - al - ize.

Such a hu-man waste._____ you're eyes __ with-out a face._

You know _ it's get - ting worse._

FLESH FOR FANTASY

Words and Music by BILLY IDOL
and STEVE STEVENS

There's a change of pace, ___ of fan-ta-sy ___ and ___

___ taste.

Do you like good mu-sic? Do you like to dance?

Oh yeah. Hang-in' out for a bod-y shop at night, ain't it strange what we do to feel all

right? Oh yeah, so

when will you call? _ I'm ex- per- i- enced. _____

_____ Oh yeah. _____ Face to _ face _ and

back to _ back, _ you see and _ feel _ my sex at- tack. _ Sing it!

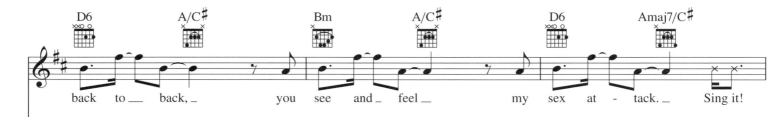

Flesh, flesh _ for fan- ta- sy. _

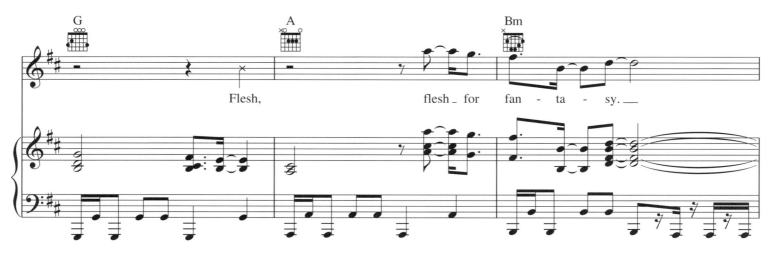

We want ___ flesh, flesh ___ for

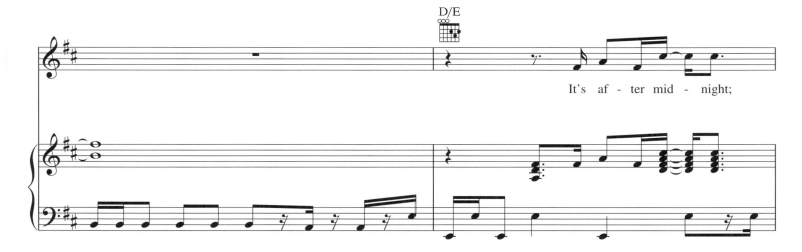

fan - ta - sy. ___

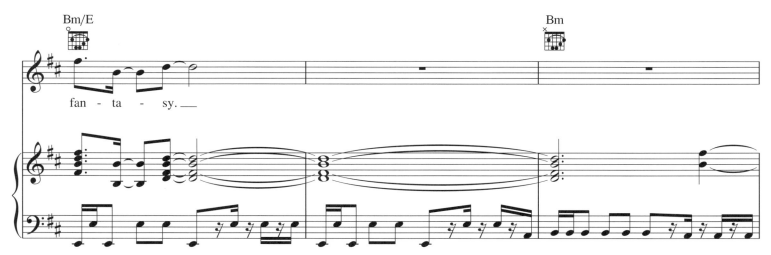

It's af - ter mid - night;

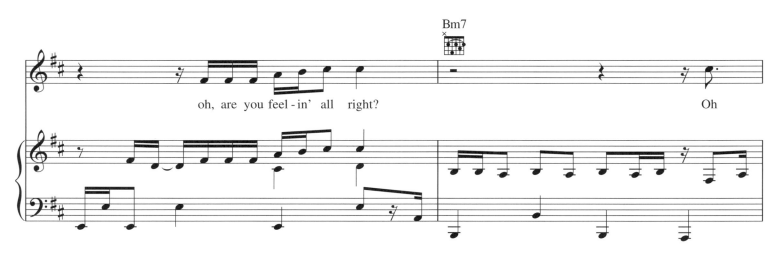

oh, are you feel - in' all right? Oh

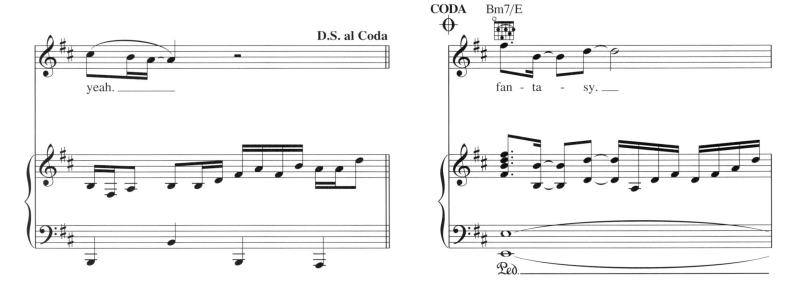

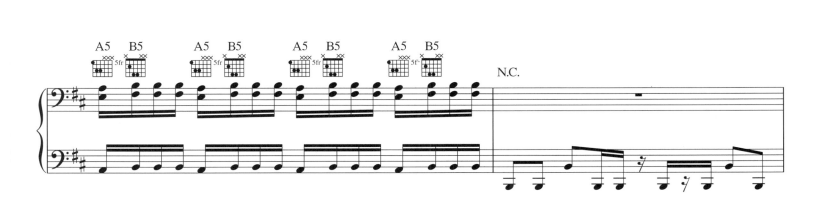

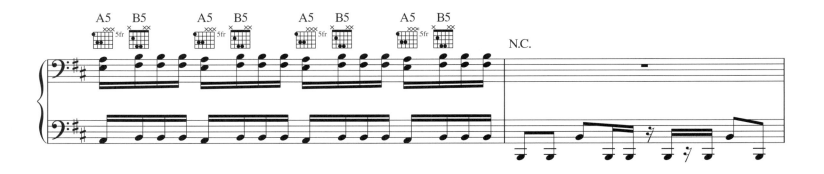

Flesh! Flesh __ for Fan - ta - sy. __

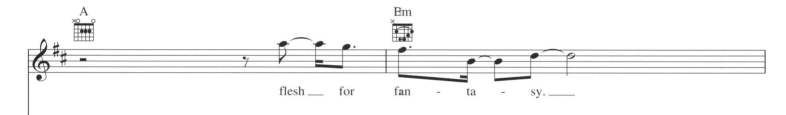

We want __ Flesh, flesh,

flesh __ for fan - ta - sy. __

We want __
You cry __ flesh,

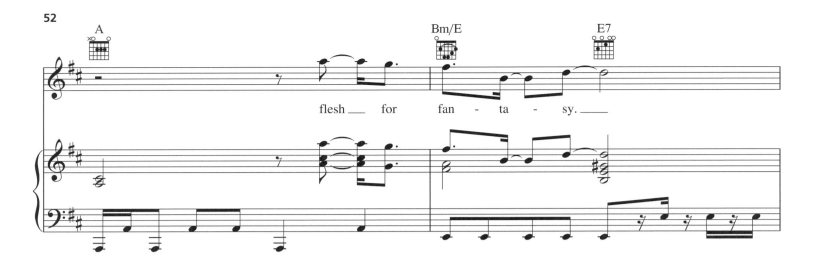

flesh ___ for fan - ta - sy. ___

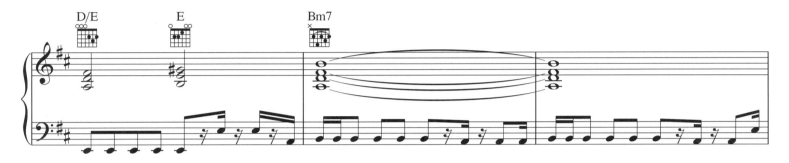

Do you like good mu - sic?   Do you like to dance? ___

___   It's near-ly morn - in'.

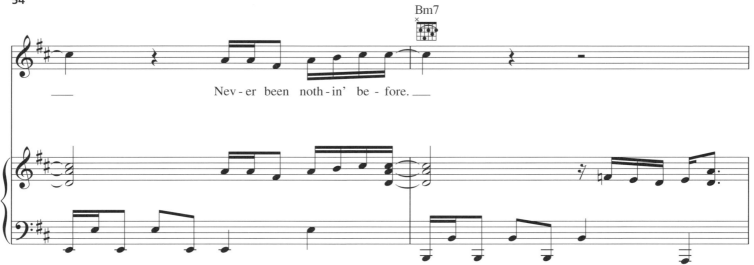

Nev - er been noth - in' be - fore.

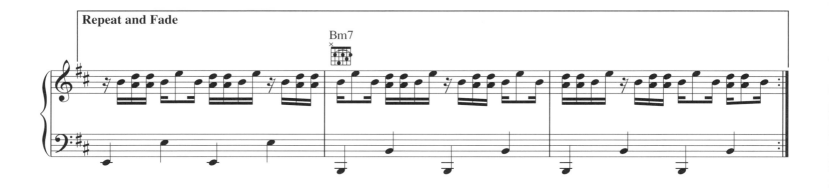

Repeat and Fade

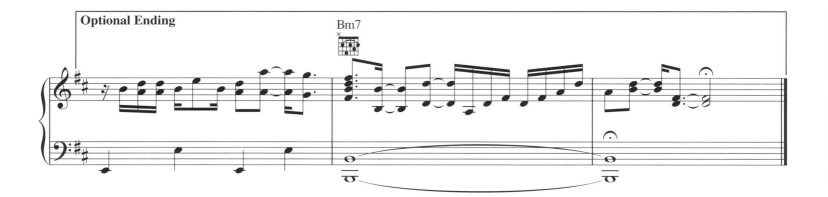

Optional Ending

CATCH MY FALL

Words and Music by
BILLY IDOL

if ___ I ___ should stum - ble. ___

Catch my fall

if ___ I ___ should

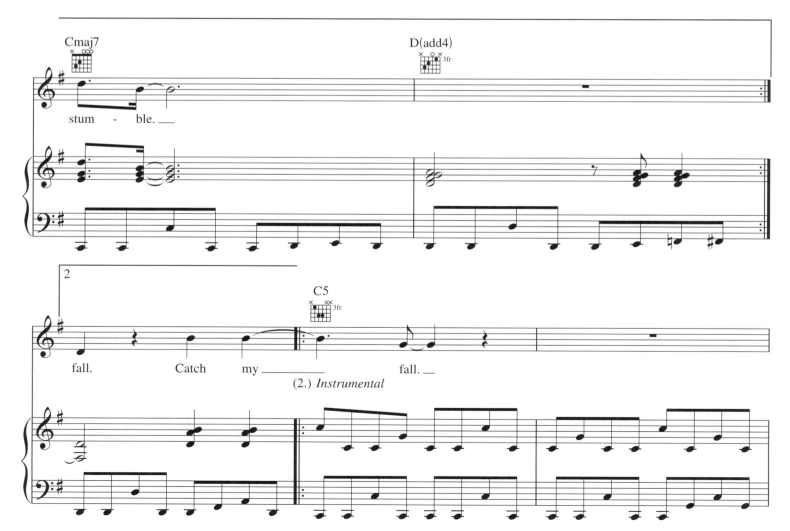

stum - ble. ___

fall.   Catch my _____ fall. ___

(2.) Instrumental

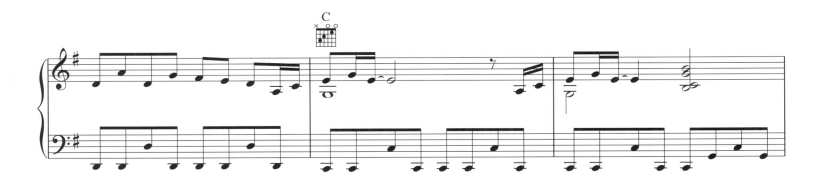

fall, yeah.

TO BE A LOVER

Words and Music by WILLIAM BELL
and BOOKER T. JONES

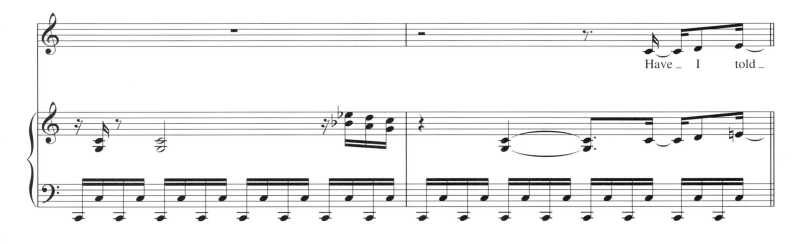

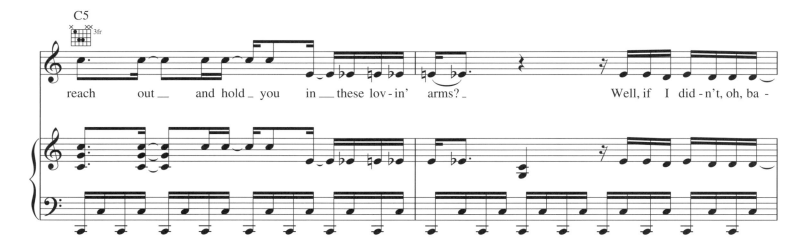

Cm/F

to be a lov - er. Have mer - cy; for-got __ to be in love with you. __

(Have

C5

C5

mer - cy.) (Have mer - cy.) (Have

For-got __ to be a lov - er. For-got __ to be a lov - er.

Cm/F

Make it on through to you __ some - how. __ I've got __ to be a lov - er, ba-

mer - cy, ba - by.) __

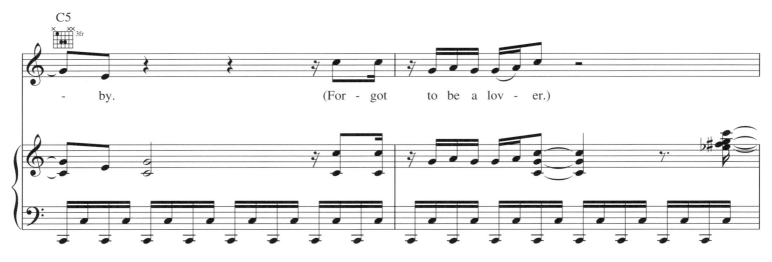

- by. (For - got to be a lov - er.)

Ooh, hoo, _ yeah, did I ask _

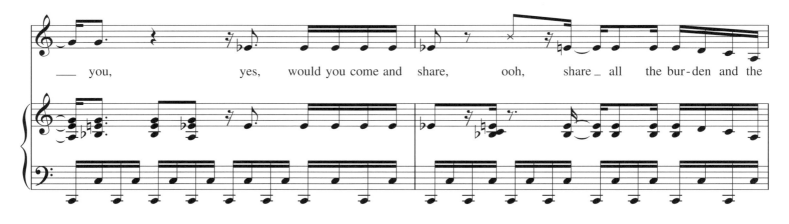

_ you, yes, would you come and share, ooh, share _ all the bur - den and the

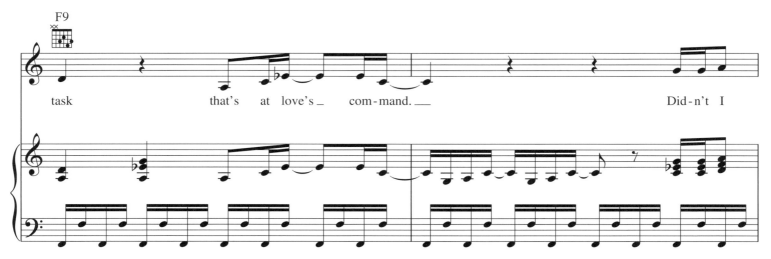

task that's at love's _ com - mand. _ Did - n't I

say all __ those lov - in', spe - cial things __ that you long __ to hear, __

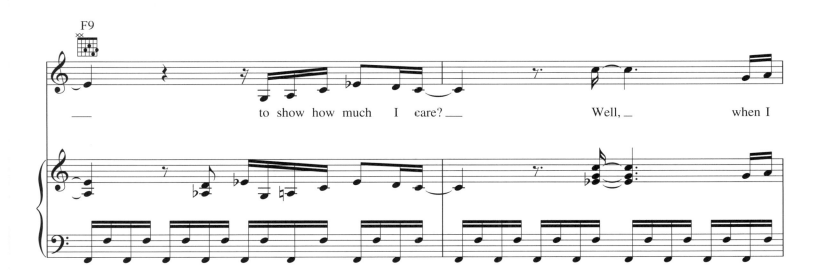

__ to show how much I care? __ Well, __ when I

(For - got

re - al - ized __ that you need love, too, gon-na spend my life __ mak-in' love __ to you. For - got

to be a lov - er.) (Have mer - cy.)
___ to be a lov - er. Have mer - cy. Well, ___ well, I

worked all day as hard ___ as I can, and worked ___ all night; ___ did-n't e-ven make ___ me a man. ___ For-got ___
(For - got

___ to be a lov - er. Have mer - cy. Ooh, ___ when I
to be a lov - er.)

re - al -ized __ you need love, too, gon-na spend my life __ mak-in' love __ to

(Got, got to be a lov - er.)

you. Got to be a lov-er, babe. __ Ooh, have

(Have mer - cy.) (Have mer - cy,

mer - cy. Have mer - cy, ba - by. I'm gon-na

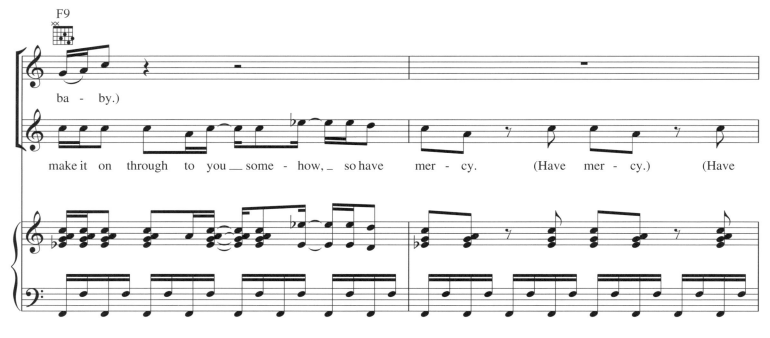

ba - by.)
make it on through to you __ some - how, __ so have mer - cy. (Have mer - cy.) (Have

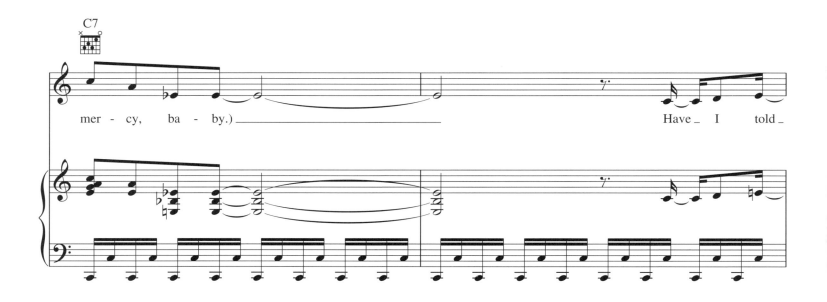

mer - cy, ba - by.) __ Have __ I told __

__ you, yes, late - ly that I love you? If I did - n't, oh, ba -

DON'T NEED A GUN

Words and Music by
BILLY IDOL

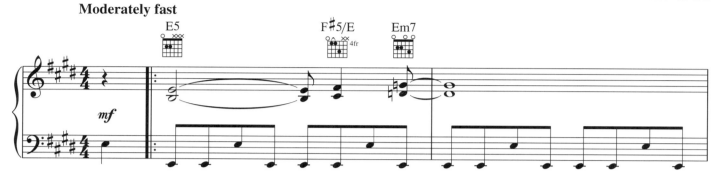

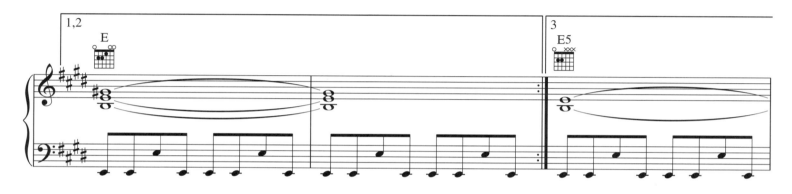

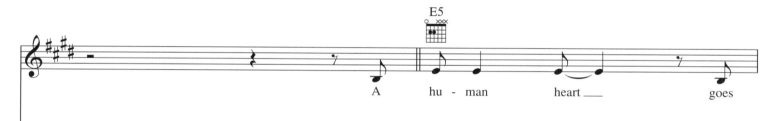

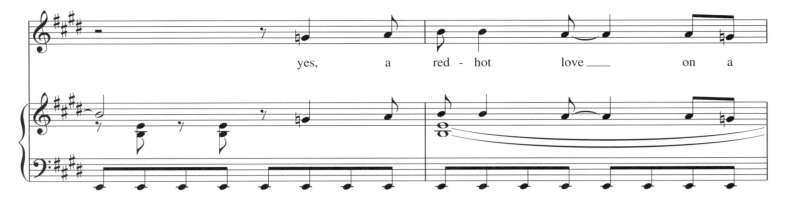

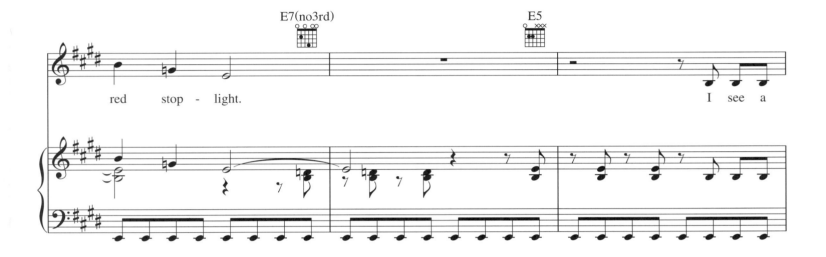

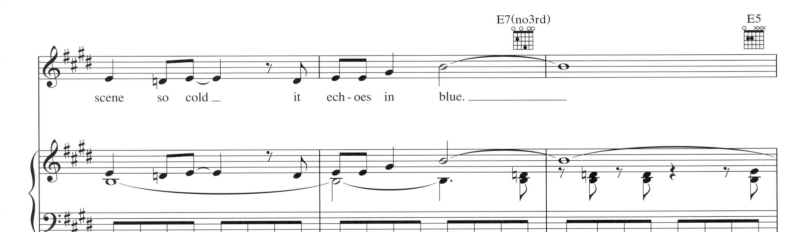

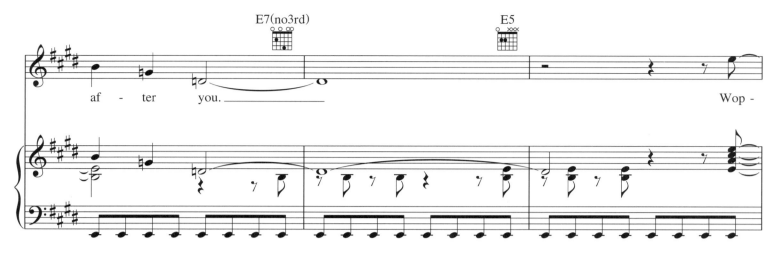

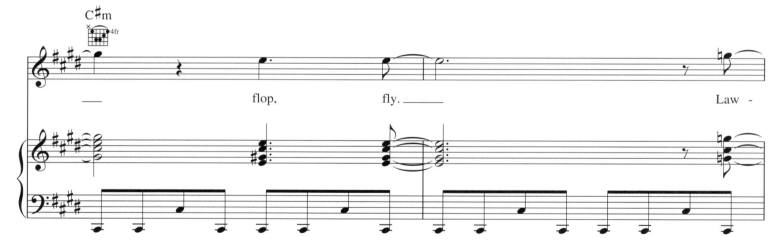

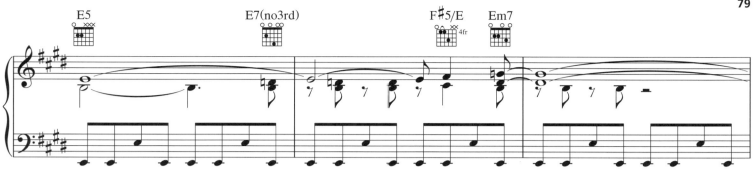

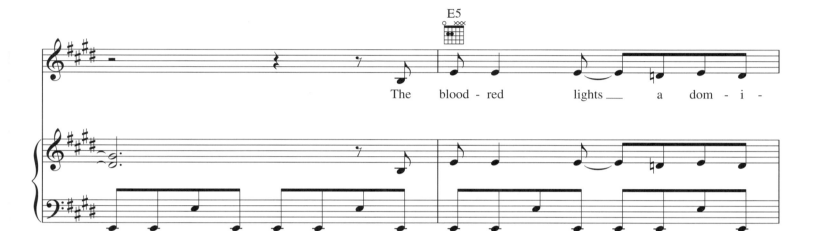

The blood-red lights __ a dom-i-

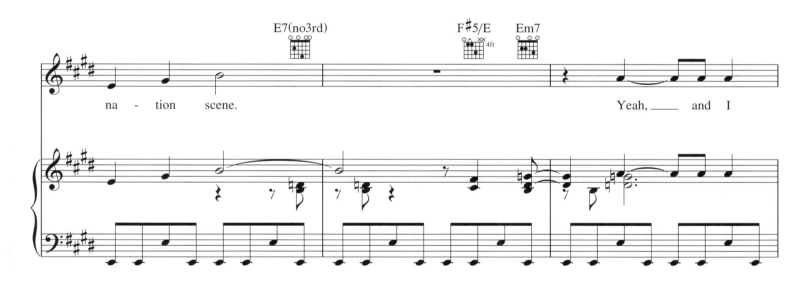

na-tion scene. Yeah, __ and I

just need your love, and to feel that __ heat. __

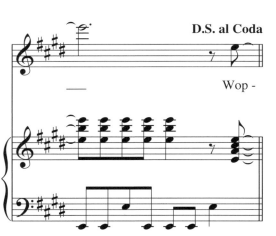

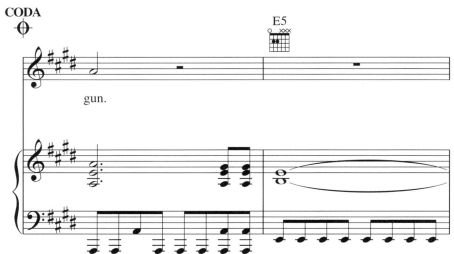

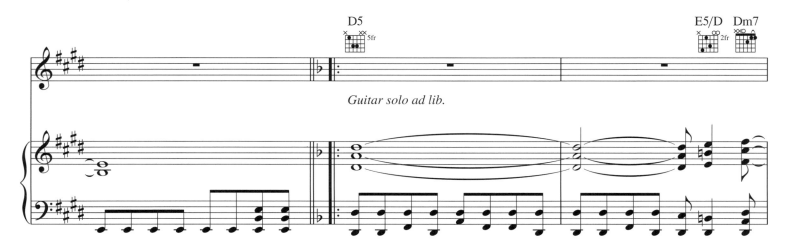

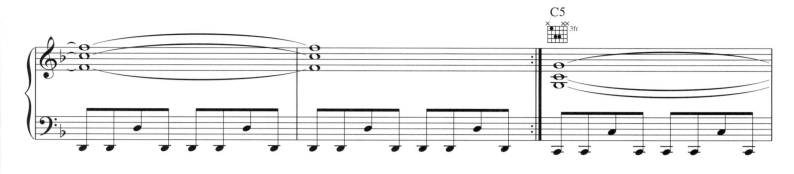

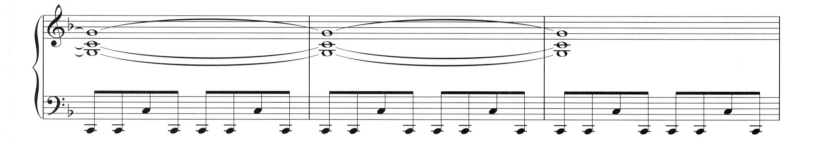

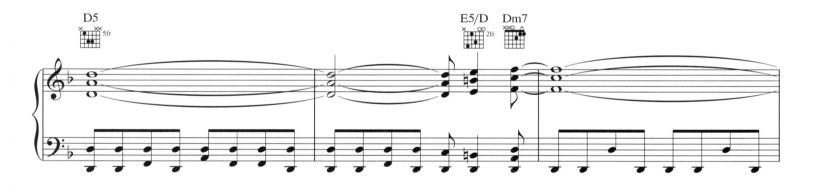

You will al - ways be cry - ing.

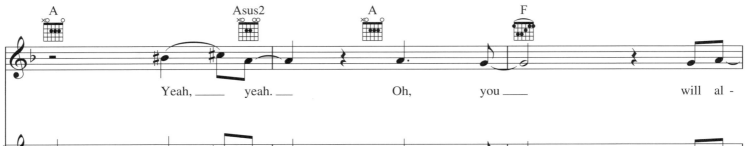

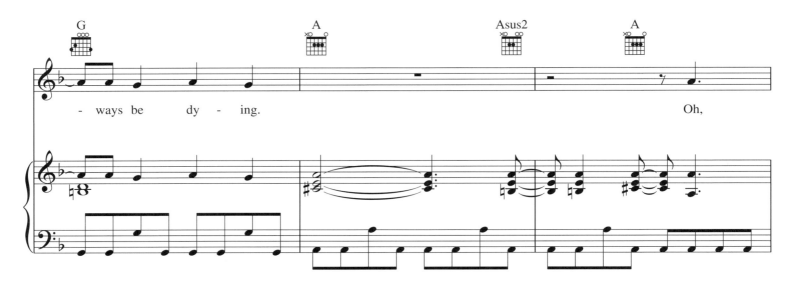

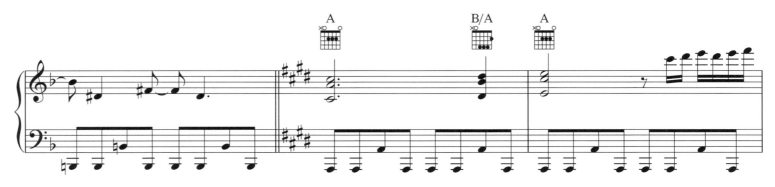

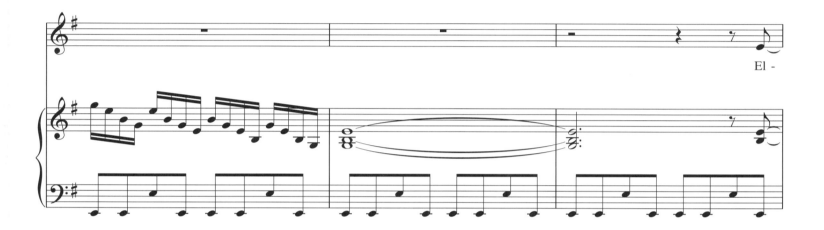

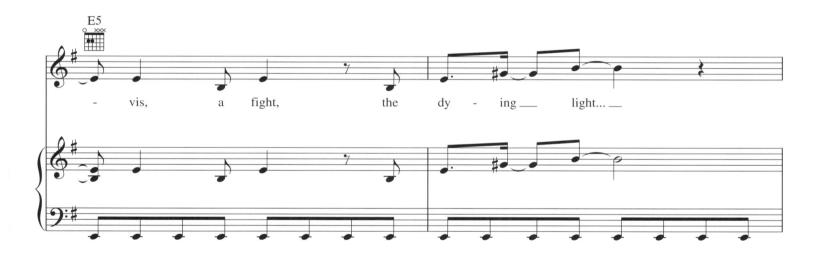

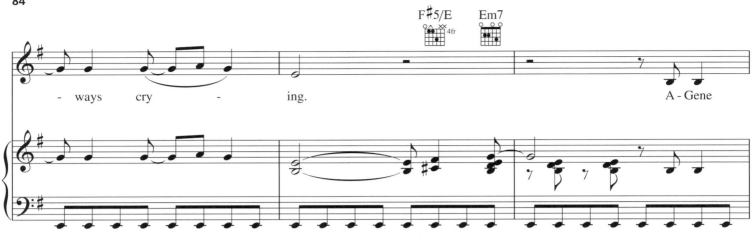

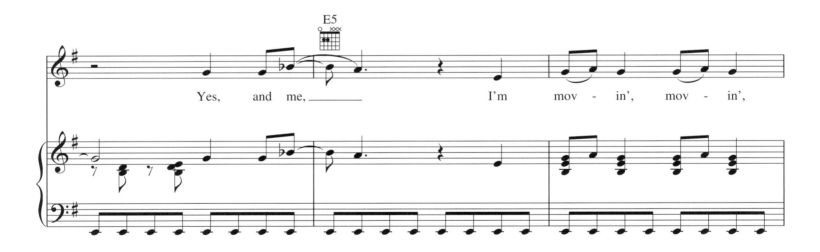

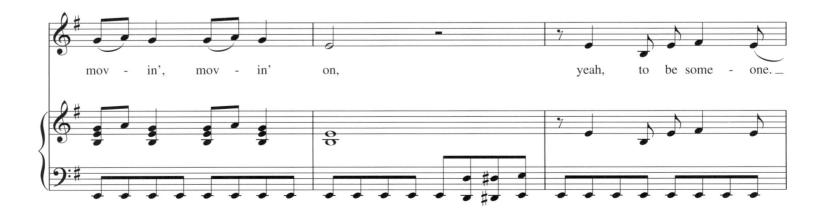

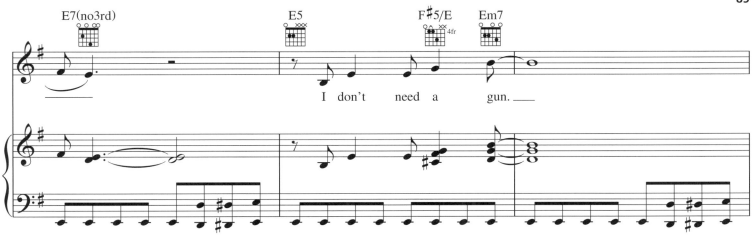

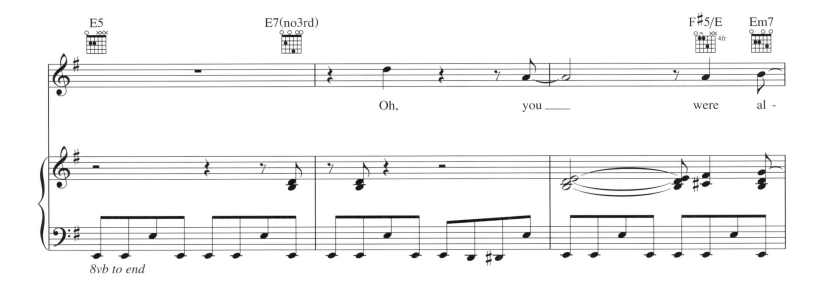

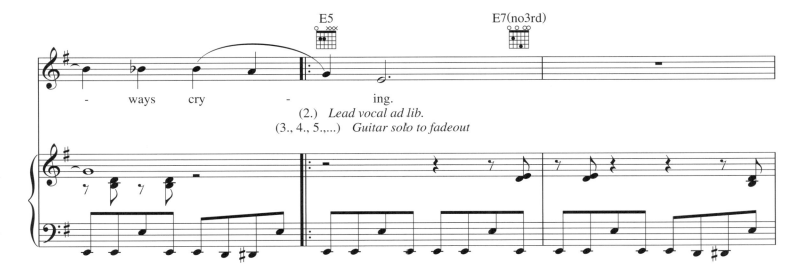

SWEET SIXTEEN

Words and Music by
BILLY IDOL

Moderately fast

Am7

mp

Am7

I'll do ___ an-y-thing for my sweet ___ six-teen, ___

{and I'll}
{oh, I'd} do ___ an-y-thing

for lit-tle run-a-way ___ child.

{Gave my heart an en-
{Well, ___ mem-o-ries will

gage - ment ring; _____ she _____ took
burn _____ you. _____ Mem - 'ries grow

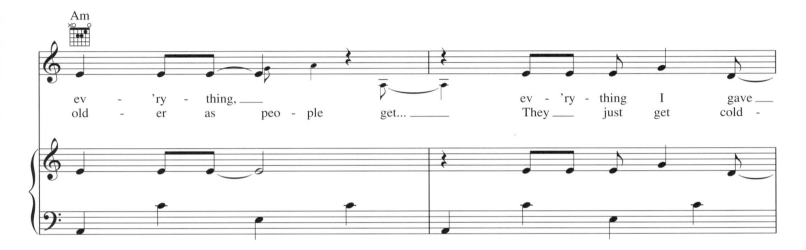

ev - 'ry - thing, _____ ev - 'ry - thing I gave _____
old - er as peo - ple get... _____ They _____ just get cold -

_____ her, oh, sweet _____ six - teen. _____
- er, like sweet _____ six - teen. _____

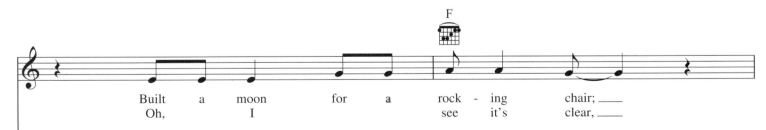

Built a moon for a rock - ing chair; _____
Oh, I see it's clear, _____

I nev-er guessed it would rock her far ___ from here. }
ba - by, that ___ you are all ___ through here. }
Oh,

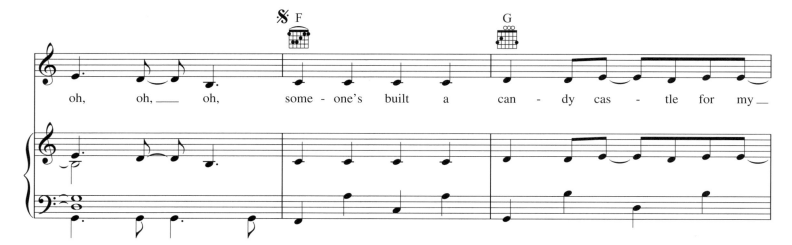

oh, oh, ___ oh, some-one's built a can-dy cas-tle for my ___

___ sweet six - teen. ___

(1.) Some - one's built a
(2.,3.) Some - one's built a

can - dy brain ___ and filled it in.
can - dy house ___ to house her in.

Well, I'll do ___ an - y -

o - ver you. ___ How, ___ how ___ do you

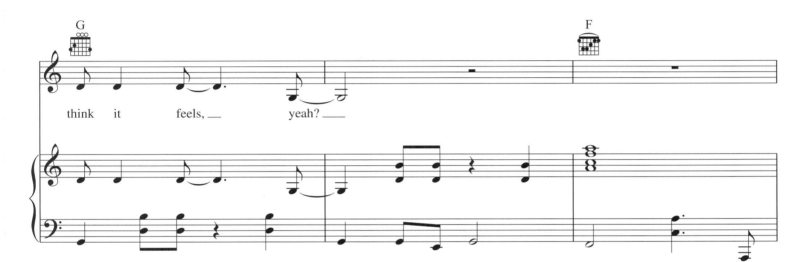

think it feels, ___ yeah? ___

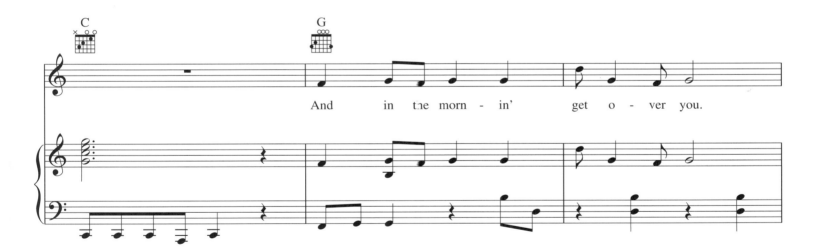

And in the morn - in' get o - ver you.

And in the morn - in' get ___ o - ver. Wipe ___ a - way the tears, ___ get ___

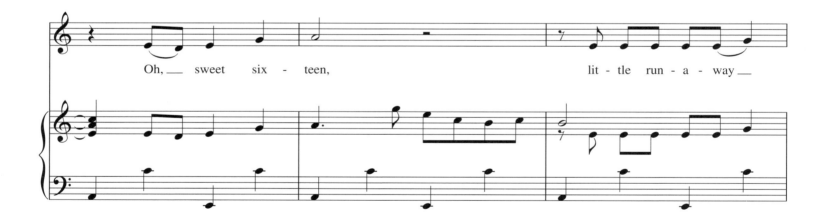

she — left ev - 'ry - thing, — ev - 'ry - thing I

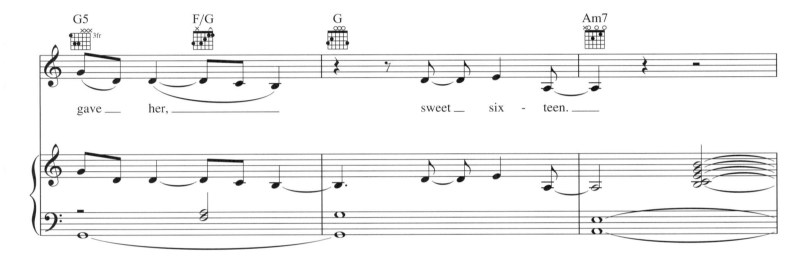

gave — her, — sweet — six - teen. —

Built a moon for a rock - ing chair; —

I nev - er guessed it would rock her far — from here.

D.S. al Coda

Eh,   mm,   mm,   oh,   oh,   oh,

CODA Am7

child?   Would do ___ an - y - thing

oh,   sweet six - teen.   I'd   do ___ an - y -

thing   for lit - tle run - a - way   girl,

95

MONY, MONY

Words and Music by BOBBY BLOOM,
TOMMY JAMES, RITCHIE CORDELL
and BO GENTRY

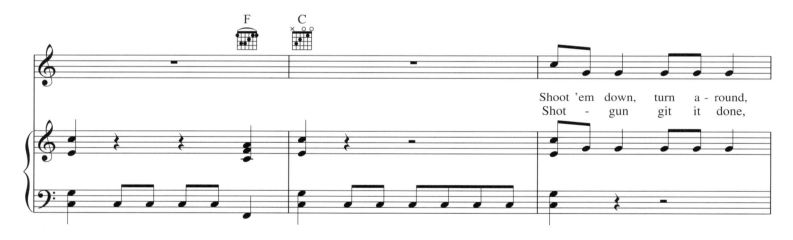

Here she comes now, say, Mo - ny, Mo - ny.
Wake me, shake me, Mo - ny, Mo - ny.

Shoot 'em down, turn a - round,
Shot - gun git it done,

come on, Mo - ny.
come on, Mo - ny.

Hey, she give me lov - in', I feel _____ all right, __ now. _____
Don't stop cook - in', it feels _____ so good, _ yeah. _____

(1.) You've got me

toss - in', turn - in' the mid - dle of the night, and I feel _____
Don't stop now. Come on, Mo - ny.

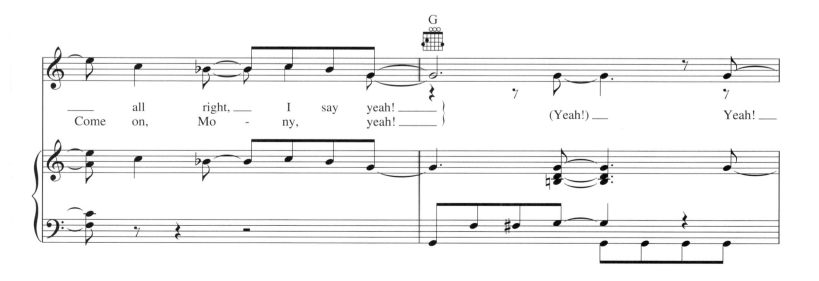

_____ all right, __ I say yeah! _____ (Yeah!) __ Yeah! __
Come on, Mo - ny, yeah! _____

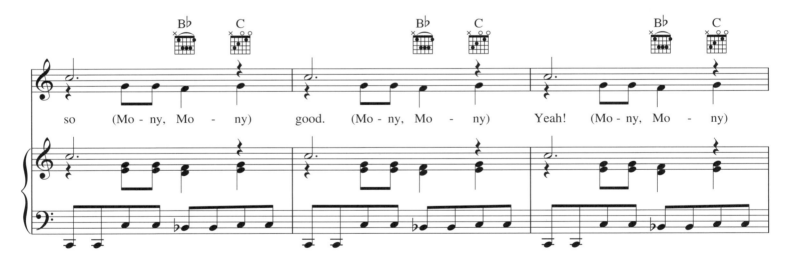

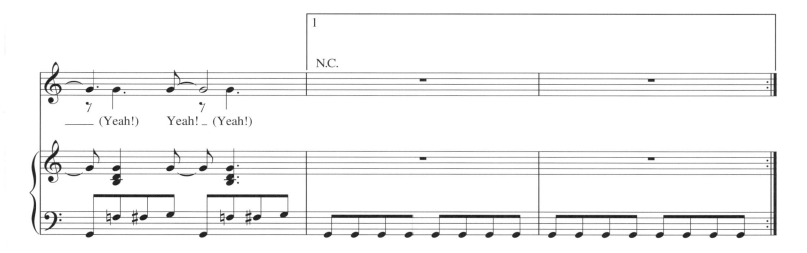

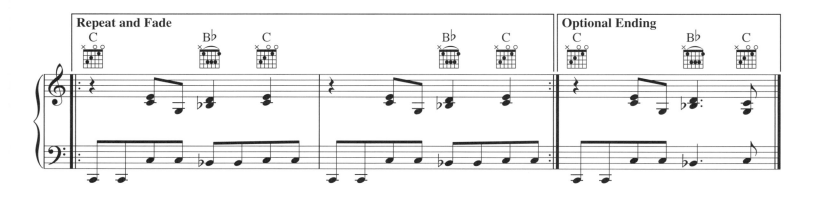

CRADLE OF LOVE

Words and Music by DAVID WERNER
and BILLY IDOL

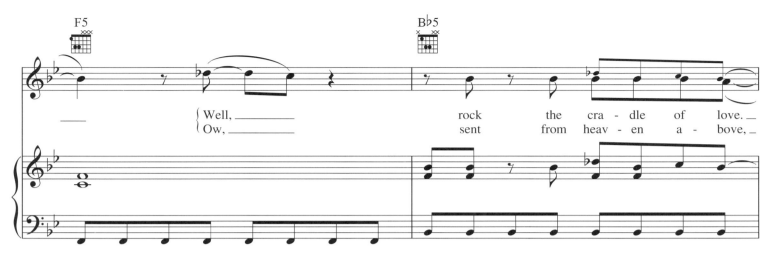

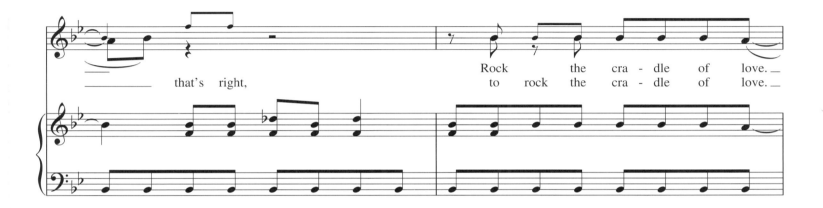

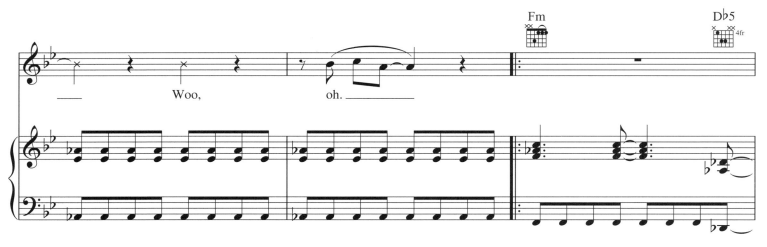

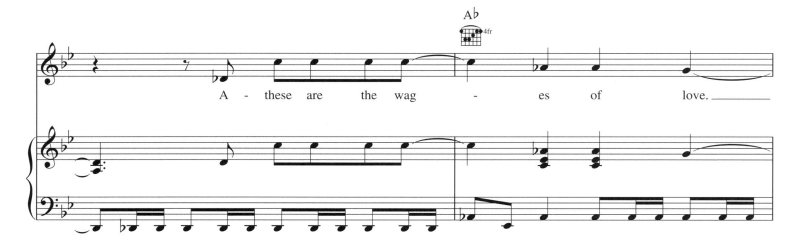

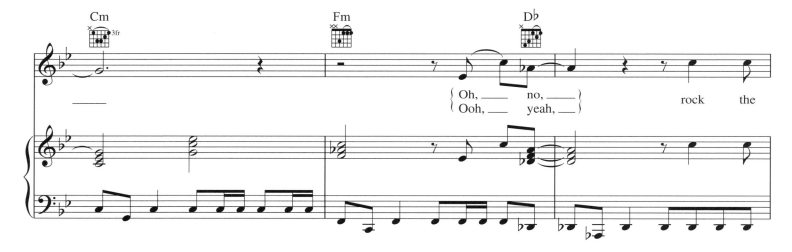

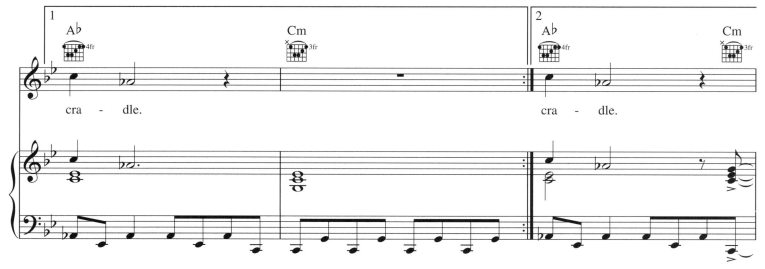

D.S. al Coda

CODA

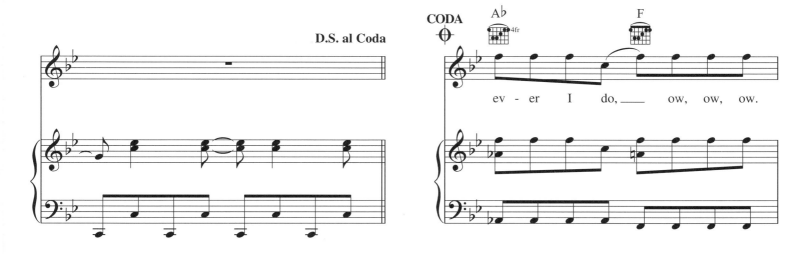

ev - er I do, ___ ow, ow, ow.

Rock the cra - dle of love, ___ yeah! Rock the cra - dle of love, __

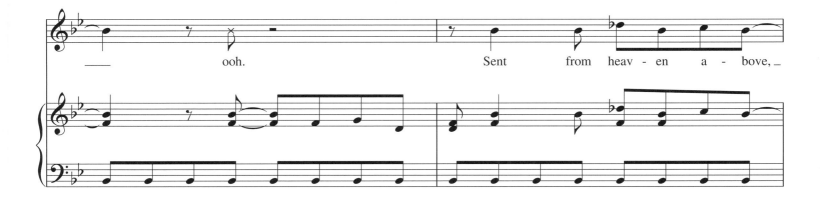

___ ooh. Sent from heav - en a - bove, __

that's right.   She rocked the cra - dle of love. _

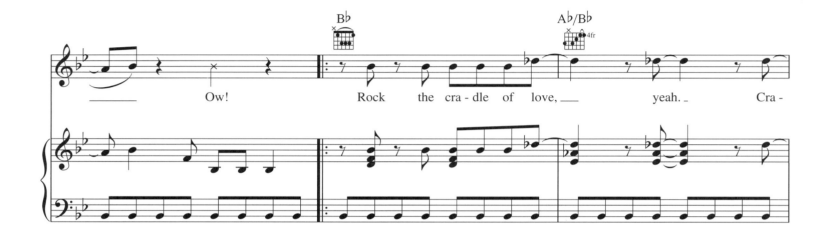

_   Ow!   Rock the cra - dle of love, _ yeah. _ Cra -

- dle of love. _   That's me, ma - ma.   I'll rob the dev - il of love. _

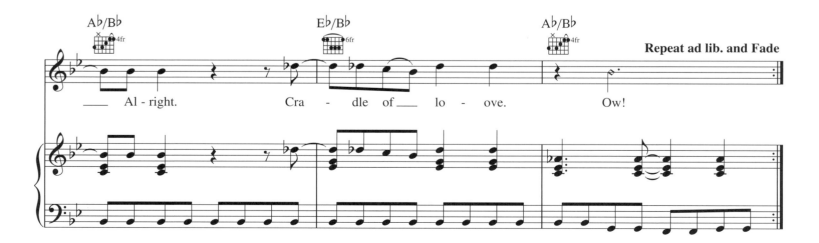

Repeat ad lib. and Fade

_ Al - right.   Cra - dle of _ lo - ove.   Ow!

L.A. WOMAN

Words and Music by
THE DOORS

Moderately fast Rock

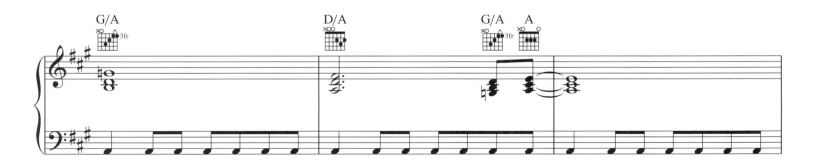

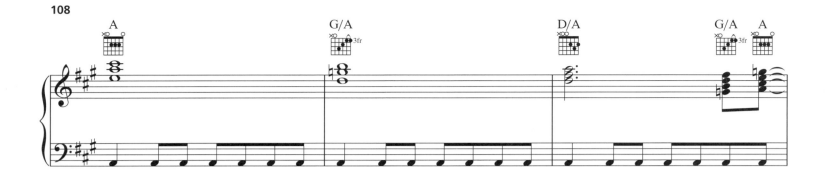

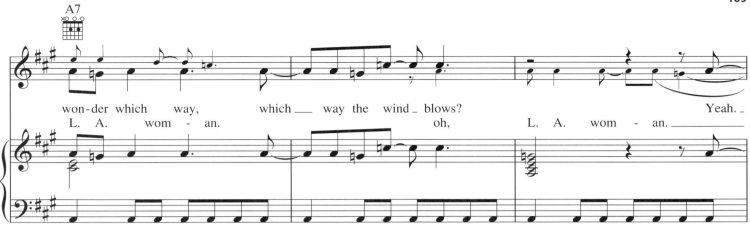

won-der which way, which _ way the wind _ blows? Yeah. _
L. A. wom - an. oh, L. A. wom - an. _

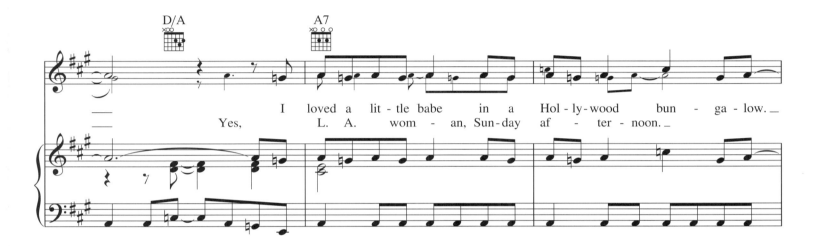

_ I loved a lit - tle babe in a Hol - ly - wood bun - ga - low. _
_ Yes, L. A. wom - an, Sun - day af - ter - noon. _

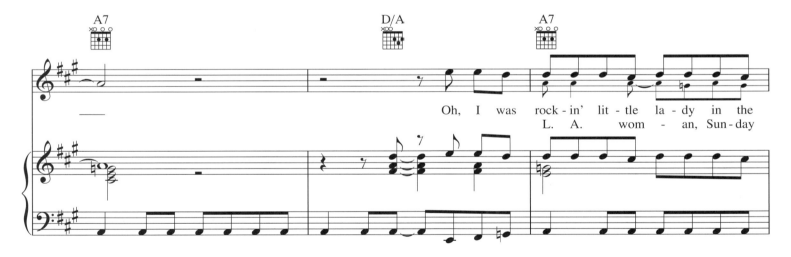

_ Oh, I was rock - in' lit - tle la - dy in the
L. A. wom - an, Sun - day

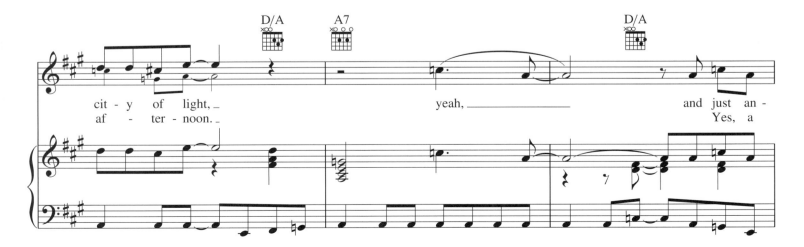

cit - y of light, _ yeah, _ and just an -
af - ter - noon. _ Yes, a

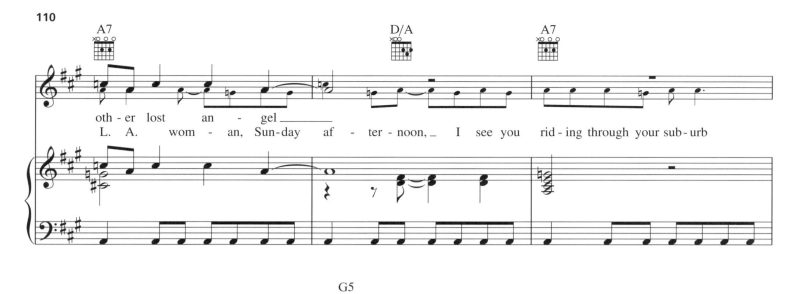

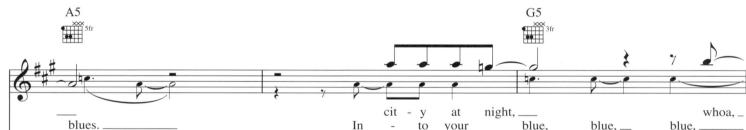

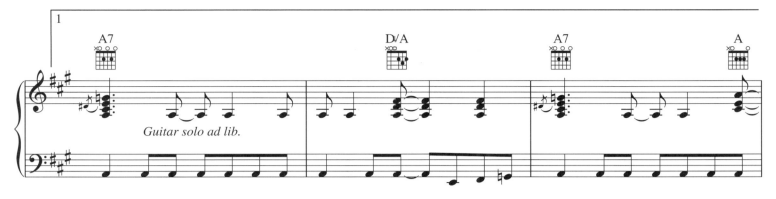

blue.

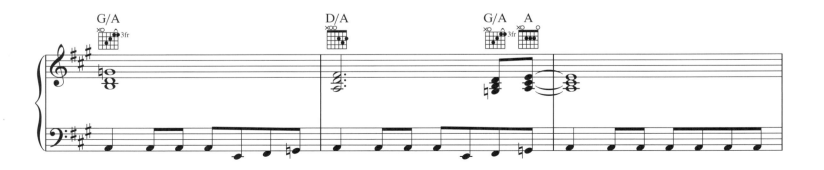

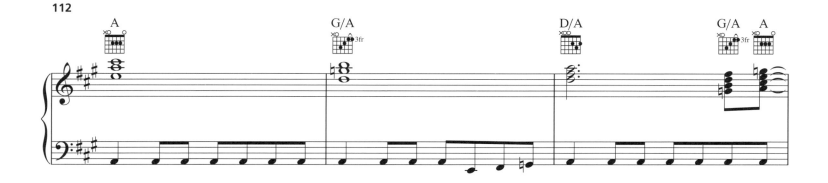

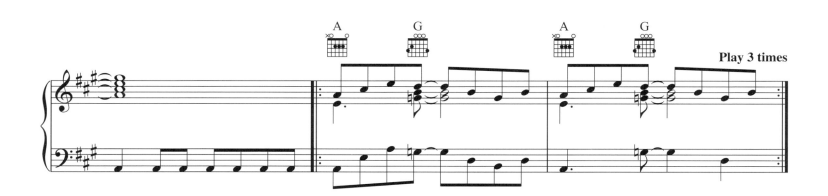

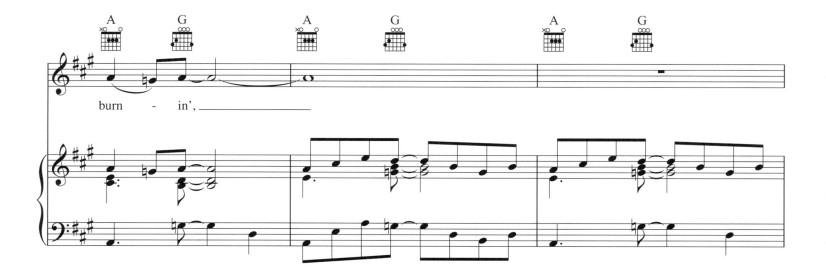

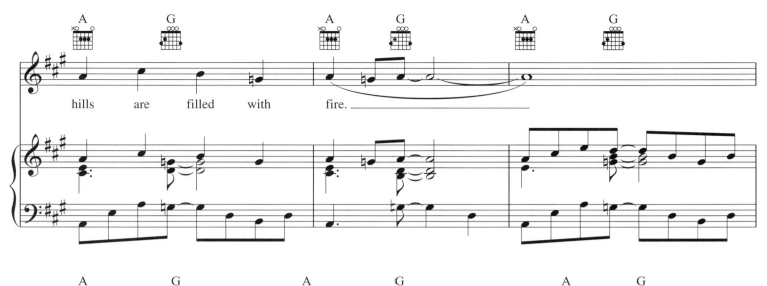

hills are filled with fire. _____

If they say I nev - er loved _____ you, _____

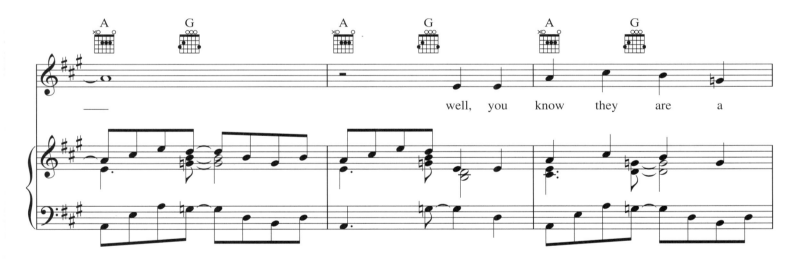

_____ well, you know they are a

li - ar. _____

Driv - in' down your free - way, __

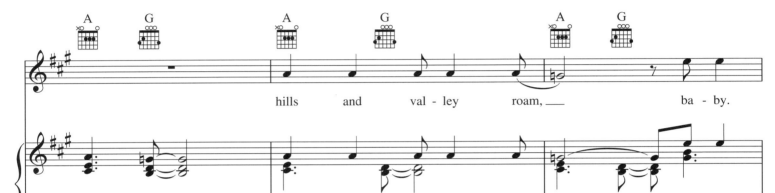

hills and val - ley roam, __ ba - by.

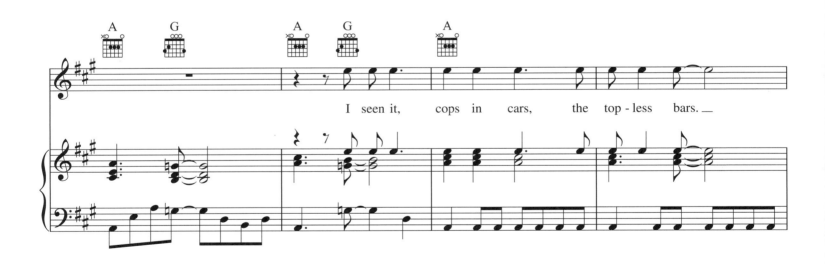

I seen it, cops in cars, the top - less bars. __

Nev - er saw a wom - an, ha, __ ha, ooh, so a - lone. __

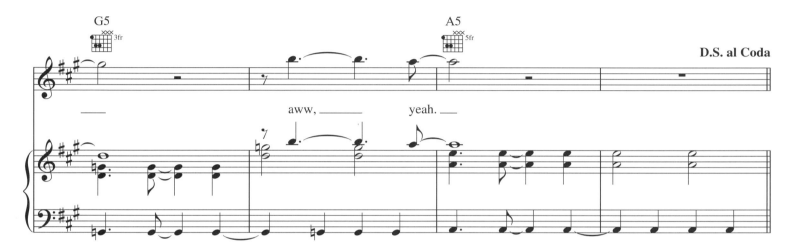

SHOCK TO THE SYSTEM

Words and Music by BILLY IDOL
and MARK YOUNGER-SMITH

It was a night, oh, what a night. L. A.
night, hell of a night. L. A., it

burn- in' bright, oh, what a night. _____
real- ly was, oh, what a ride. _____

I said, yeah, come on.

{ It make my world stand still. }
{ It make my life feel real. }

Oh, _____

Recorded a half step higher.

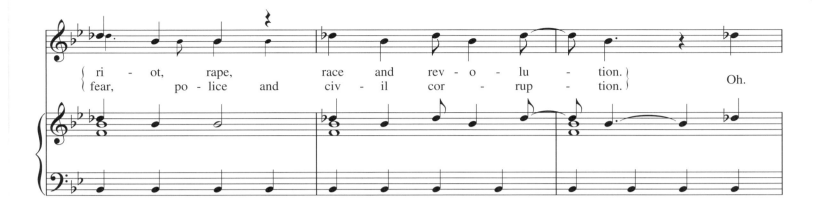

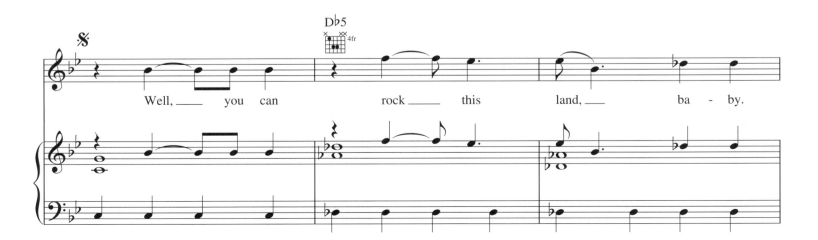

Yeow, ___ it's like a shock to the sys-

-tem. It feels good, well, al - right. ___ It's like a

shock to the sys - tem. I say yeah. ___

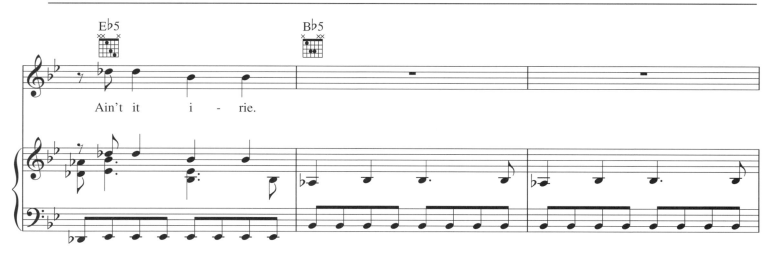

Ain't it i - rie.

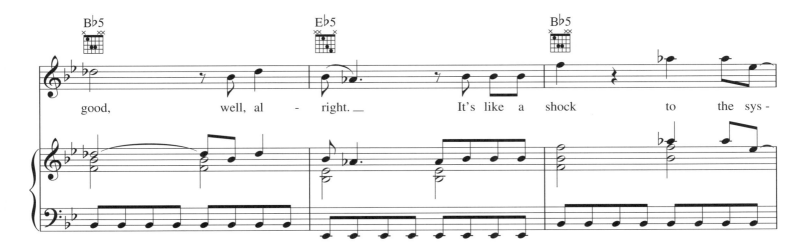

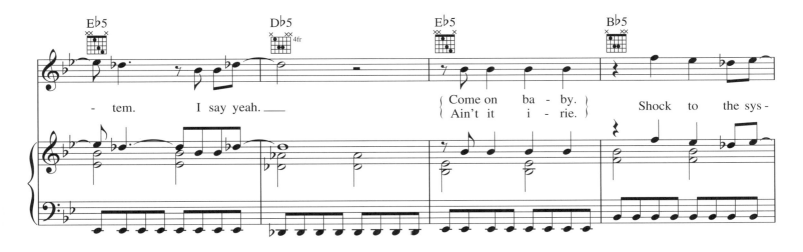

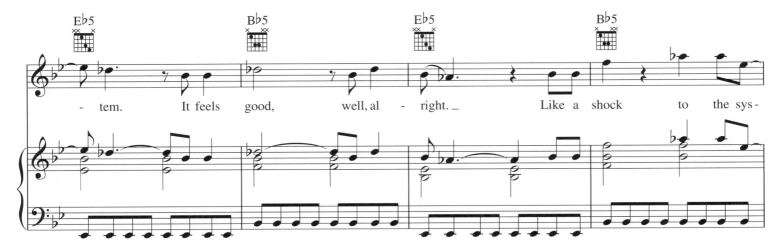

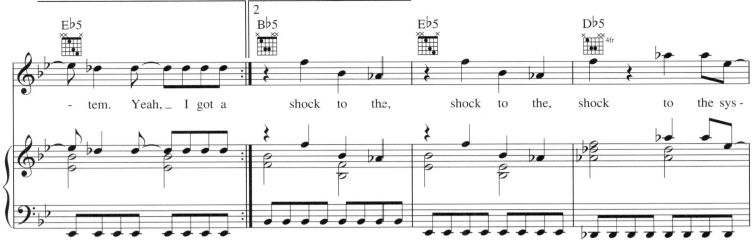

-tem. Yeah, __ I got a shock to the, shock to the, shock to the sys-

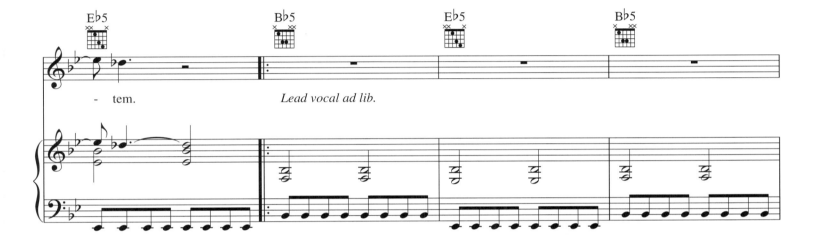

-tem. *Lead vocal ad lib.*

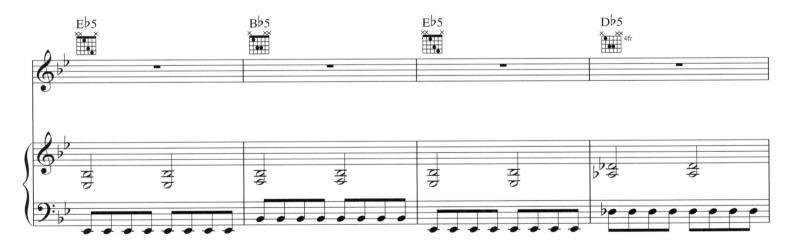

The world still burns.

SPEED
from SPEED

Words and Music by BILLY IDOL
and STEVE STEVENS

Hard driving Rock

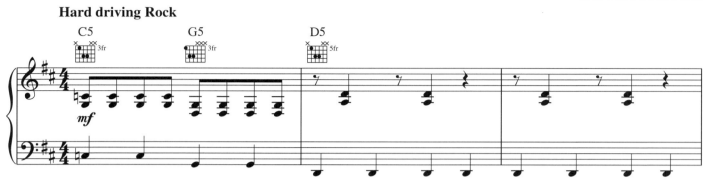

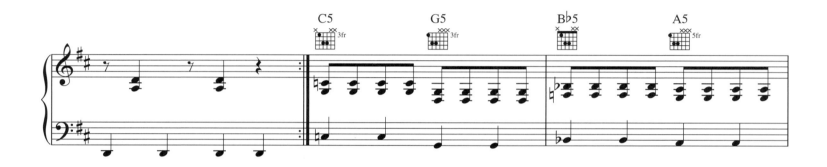

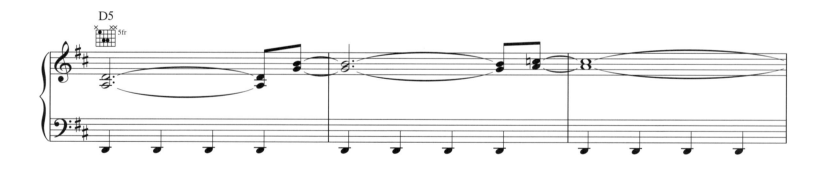

Run - nin' from the night - mare in the
train full of pain on the

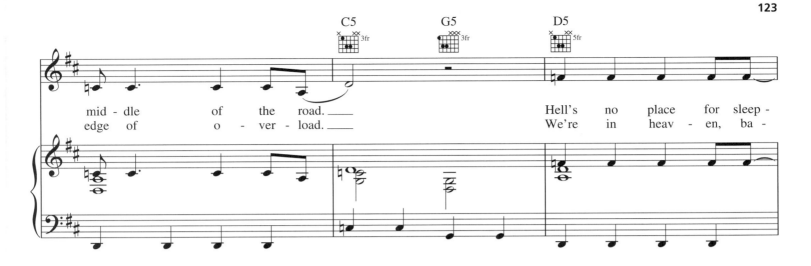

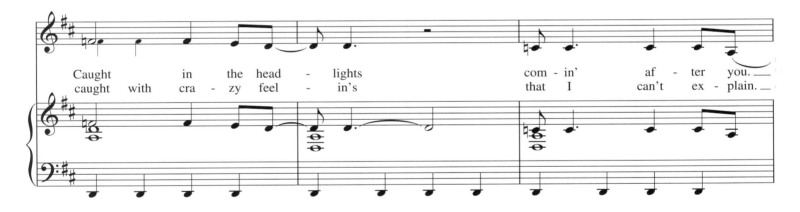

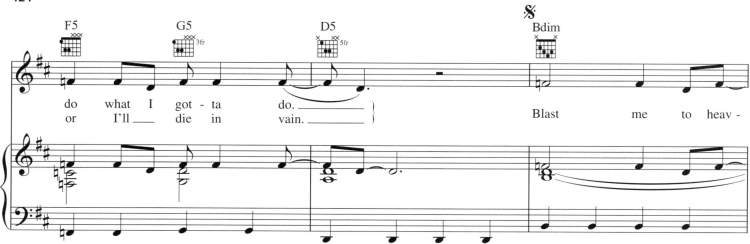

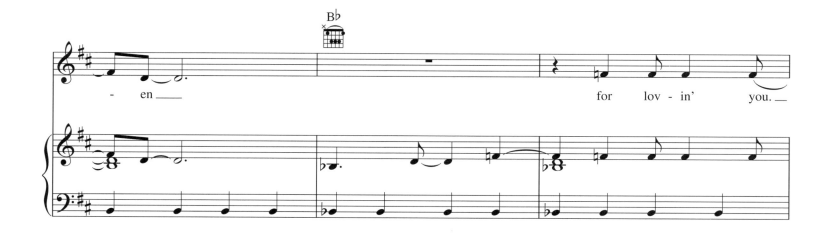

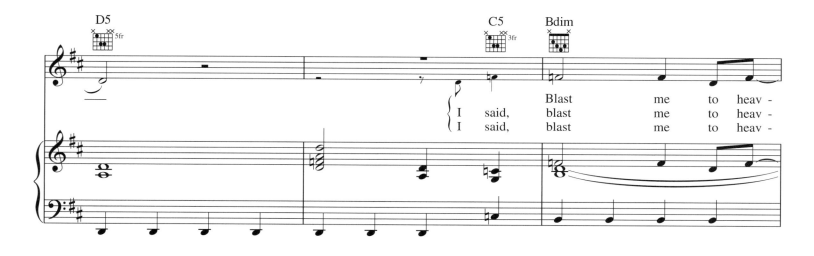

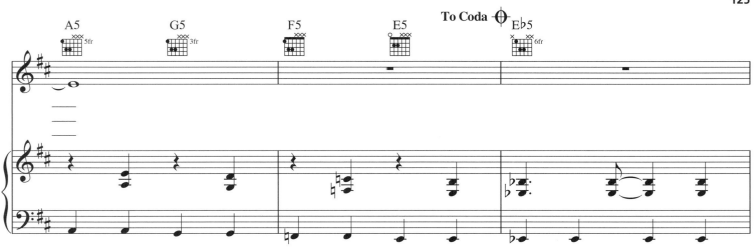

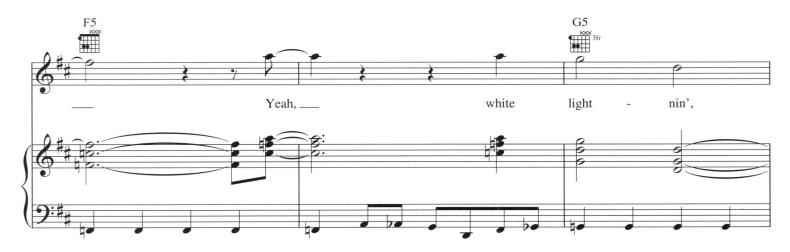

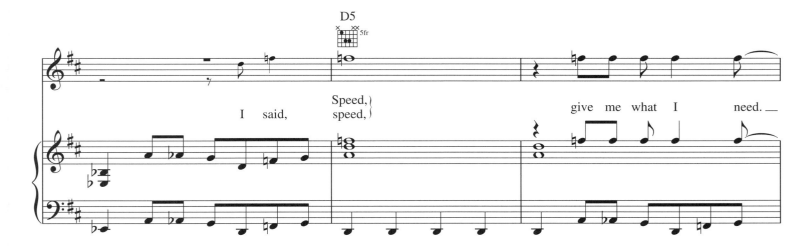

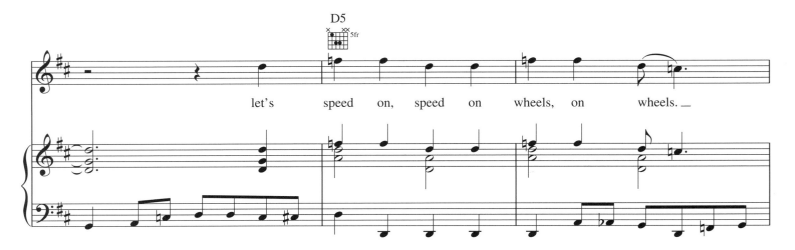

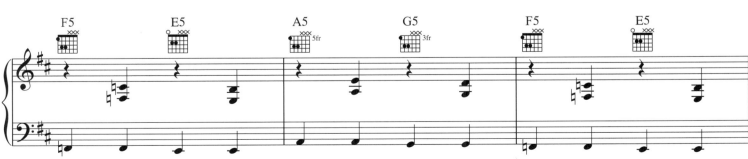

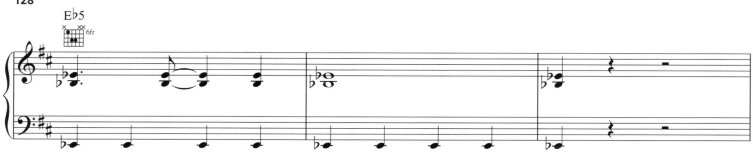

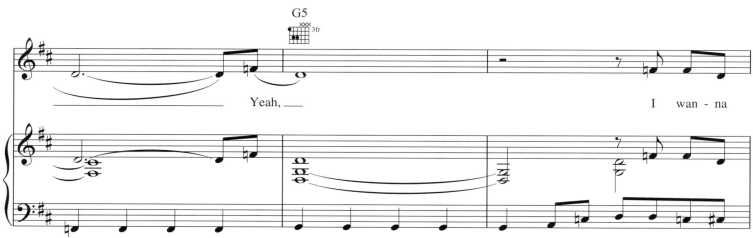

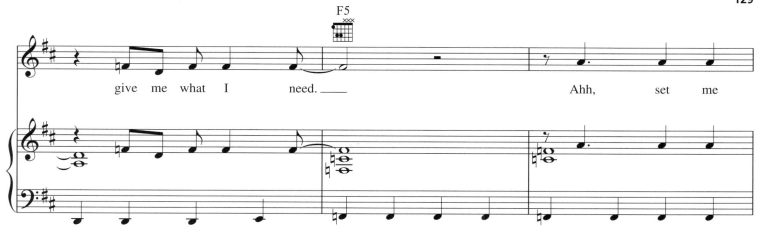

give me what I need. _____ Ahh, set me

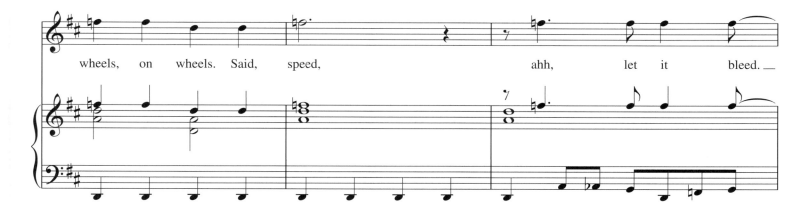

free. Let's speed on wheels, on

wheels, on wheels. Said, speed, ahh, let it bleed. __

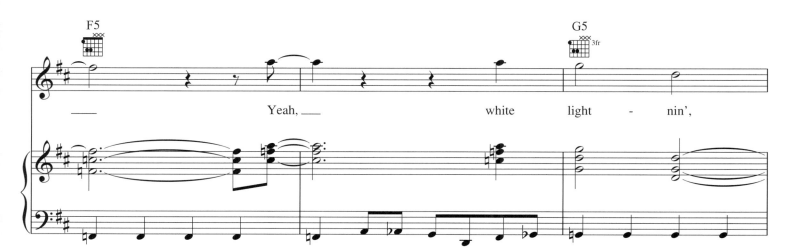

_____ Yeah, _____ white light - nin',

let's speed on, speed on wheels, on wheels.

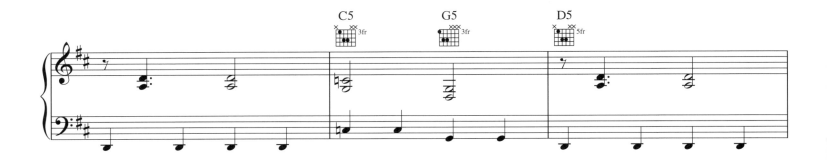

I said,

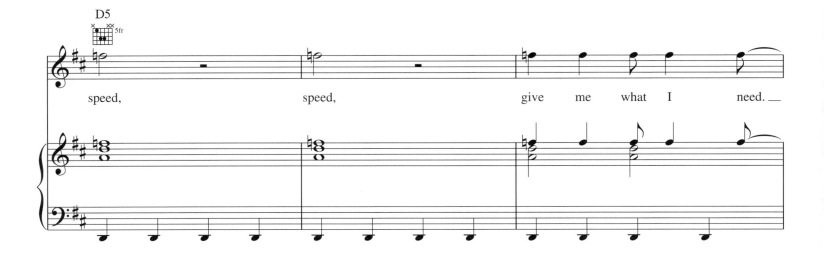

speed, speed, give me what I need. __

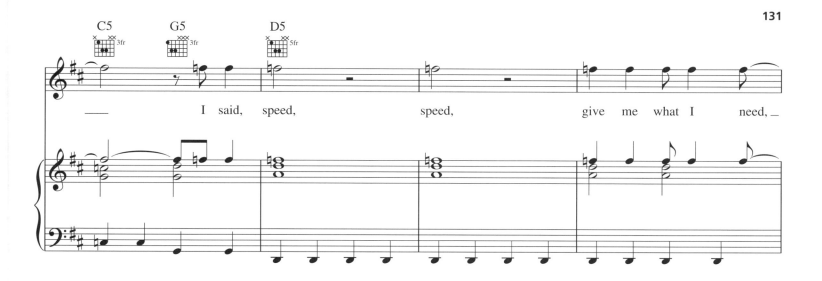

I said, speed, speed, give me what I need, _

_ al - right.

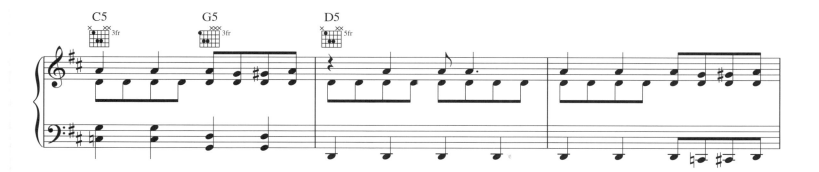

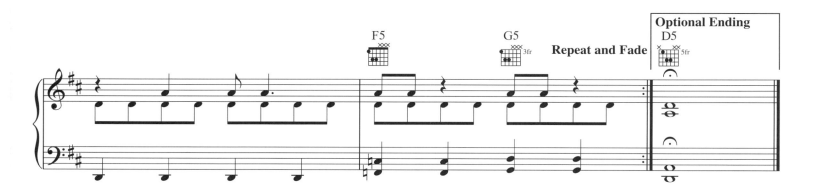

WORLD COMIN' DOWN

Words and Music by BILLY IDOL
and BRIAN TICHY

Fast, driving Rock

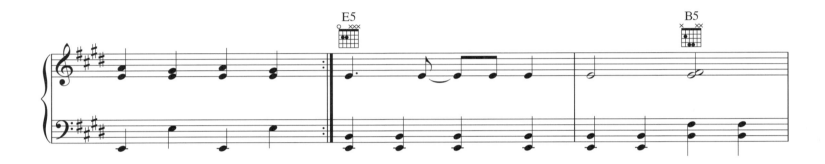

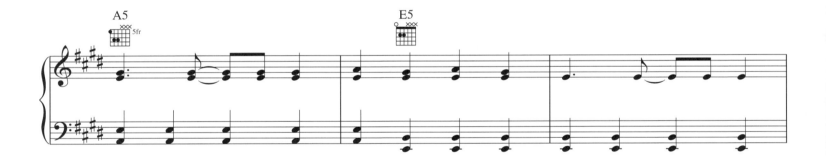

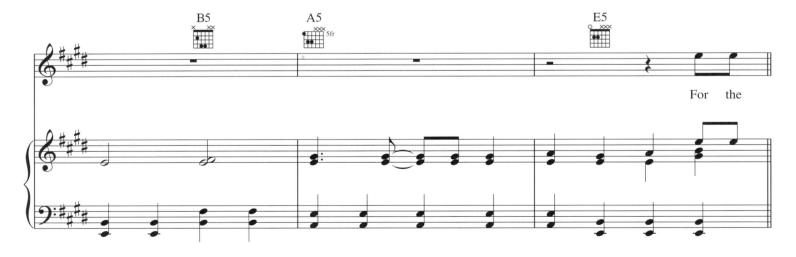

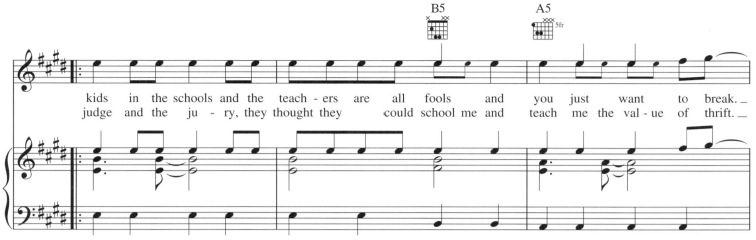

kids in the schools and the teach-ers are all fools and you just want to break. ___
judge and the ju-ry, they thought they could school me and teach me the val-ue of thrift. ___

___ I said, you're close to the edge and you're pissed at your work and the
___ They put me in-side on a one to five and

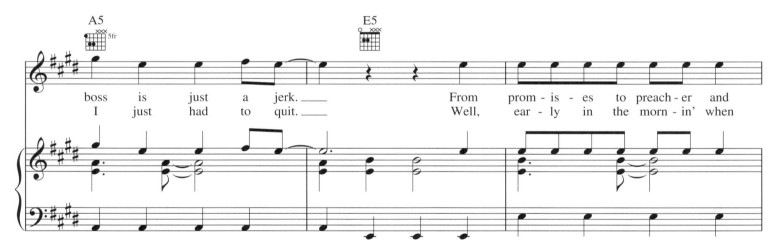

boss is just a jerk. ___ From prom-is-es to preach-er and
I just had to quit. ___ Well, ear-ly in the morn-in' when

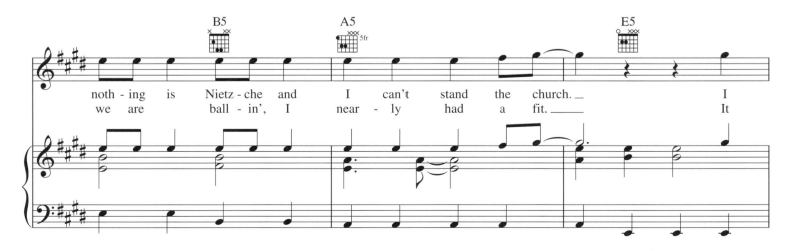

noth-ing is Nietz-che and I can't stand the church. ___ I
we are ball-in', I near-ly had a fit. ___ It

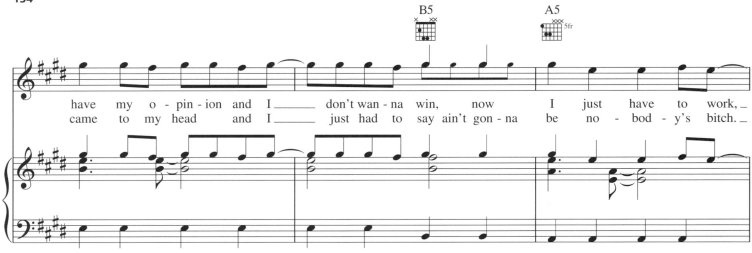

have my o-pin-ion and I ____ don't wan-na win, now I just have to work, ___
came to my head and I ____ just had to say ain't gon-na be no-bod-y's bitch. ___

____ al - right. ___ Well, I feel the whole world ___

____ com-in' down ____ on me. ____

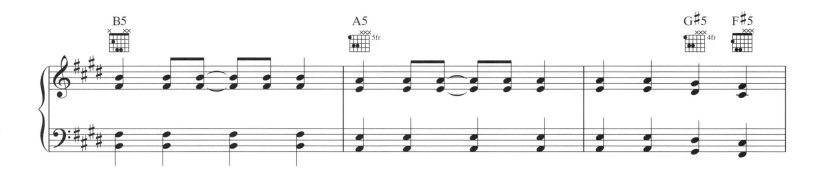

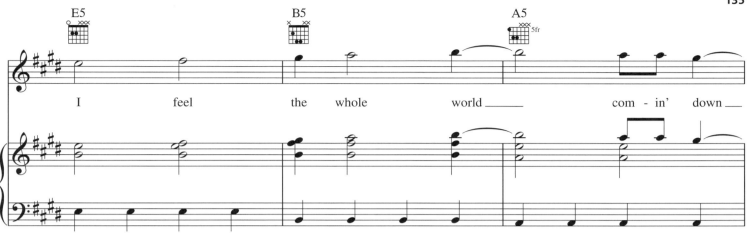

I feel the whole world _____ com - in' down _____

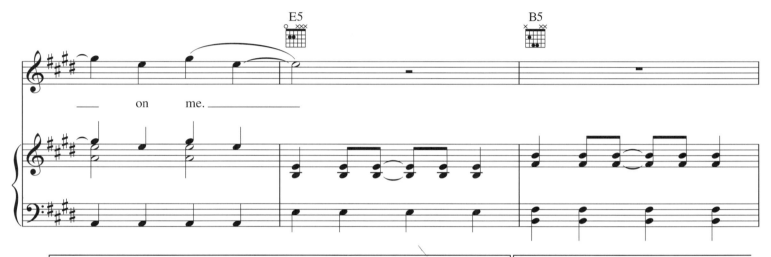

_____ on me. _____

Well, the

Com - in' down, _____ down on

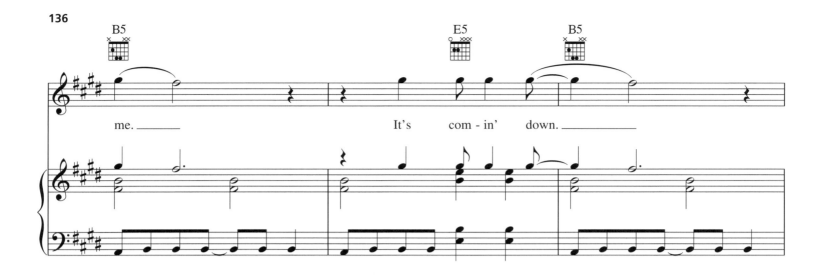

me. _____ It's com - in' down. _____

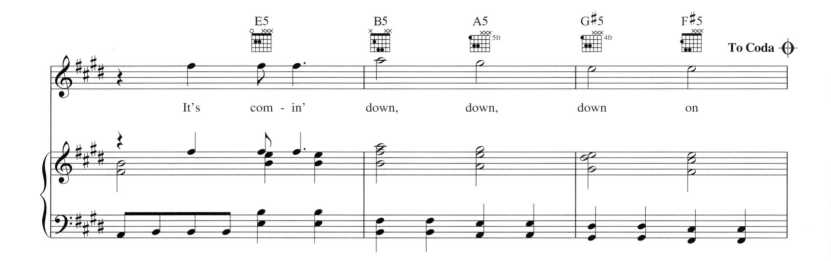

It's com - in' down, down, down on

To Coda ⊕

me.

There's on-ly one thing that I ___

___ can do now, go lie in the sun. _____ I wan-na

soak up the rays and burn ___ my-self black 'cause can-cer day has

come. Ev-'ry-thing you do to pro-tect your-self, ___ well, it

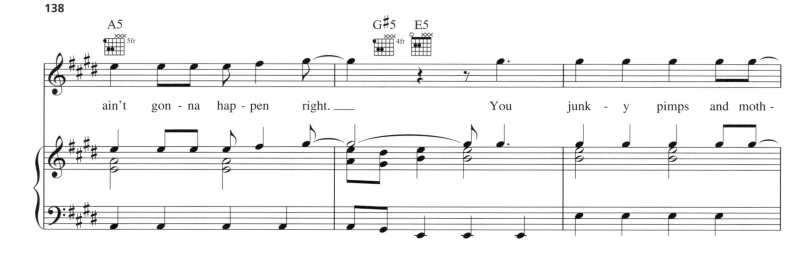

ain't gon - na hap - pen right. ___ You junk - y pimps and moth -

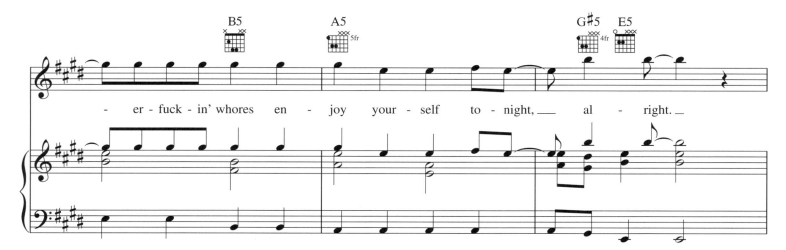

- er - fuck - in' whores en - joy your - self to - night, ___ al - right. ___

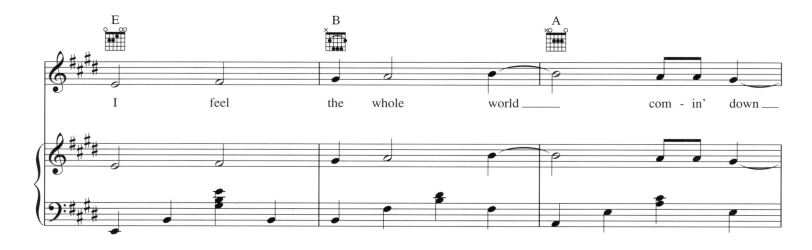

I feel the whole world _____ com - in' down ___

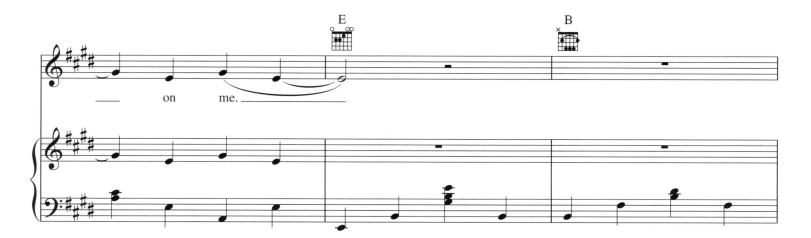

___ on me. _____

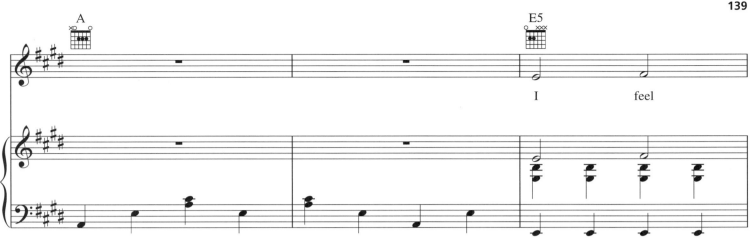

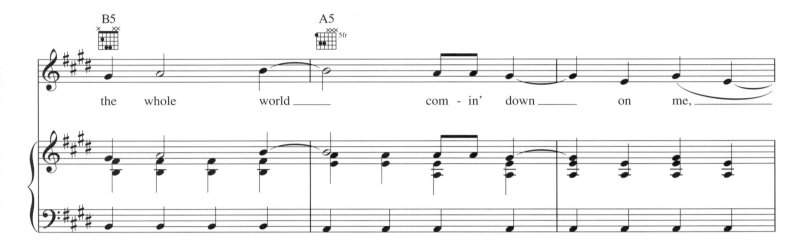

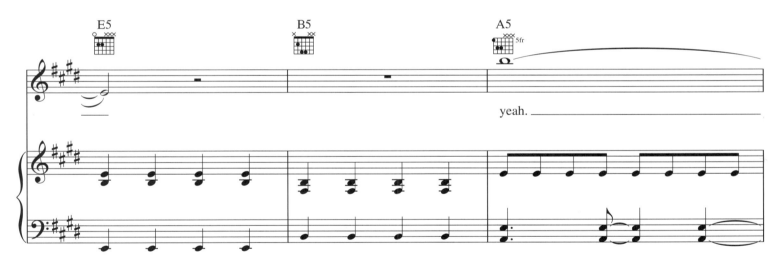

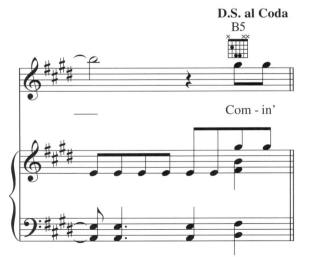

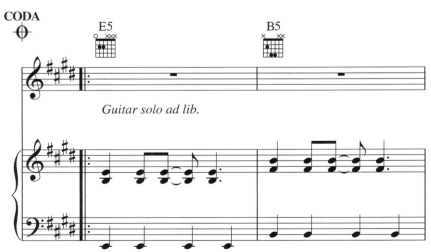

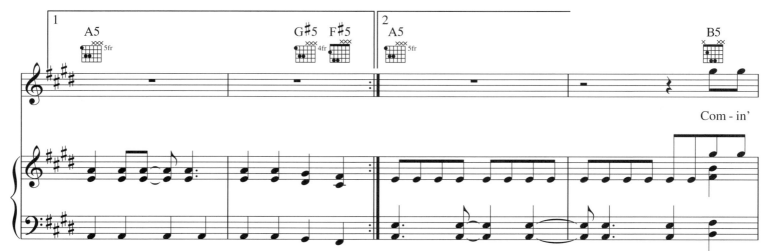

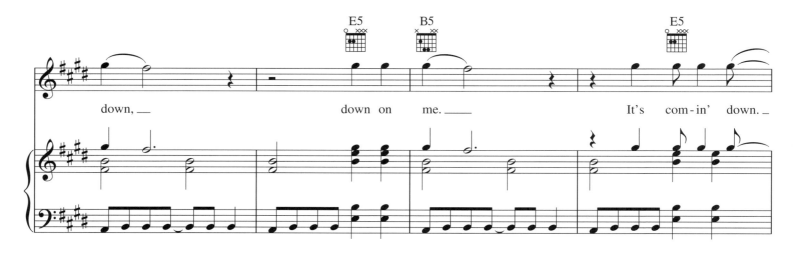

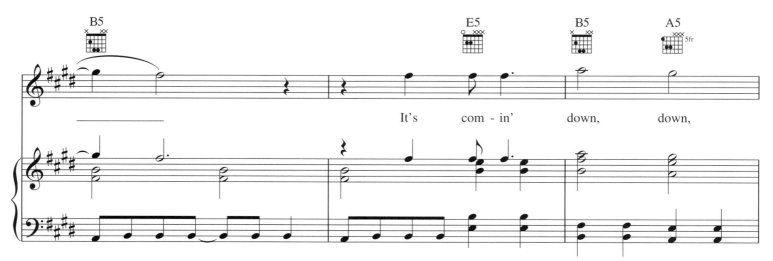

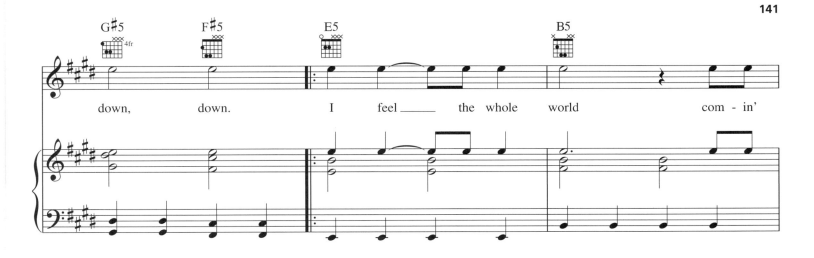

down, down. I feel _____ the whole world com - in'

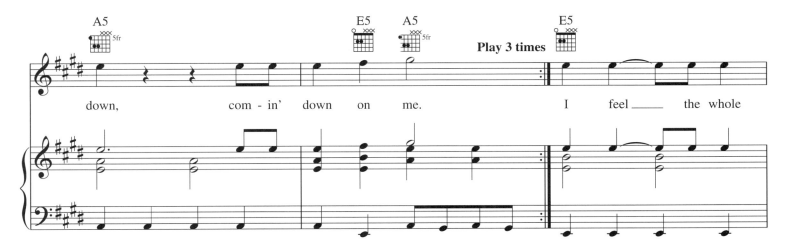

Play 3 times

down, com - in' down on me. I feel _____ the whole

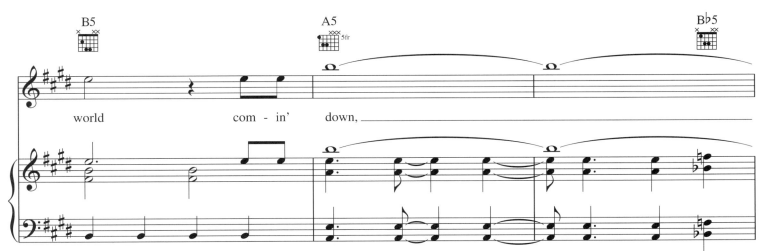

world com - in' down, _____

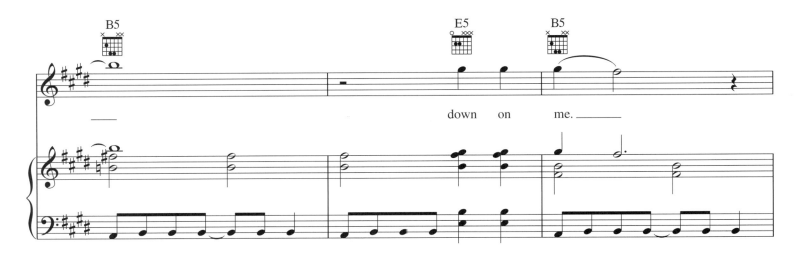

_____ down on me. _____

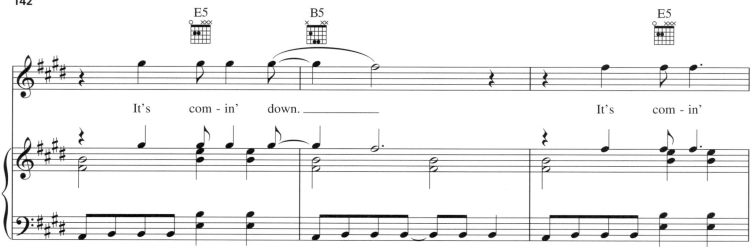

It's com-in' down. _____ It's com-in'

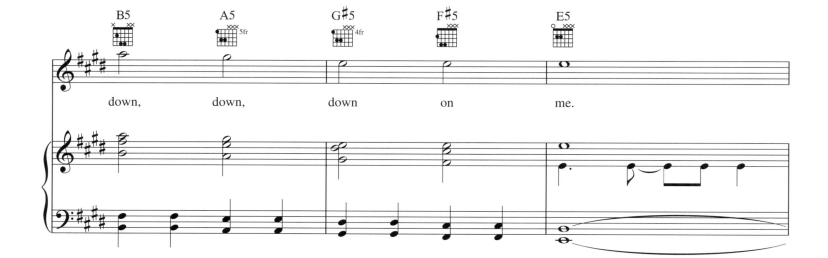

down, down, down on me.

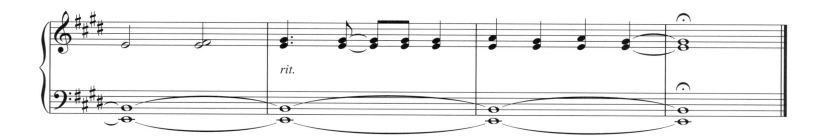

rit.

JOHN WAYNE

Words and Music by BILLY IDOL,
BRIAN TICHY and DEREK SHERINIAN

Intense Rock feel

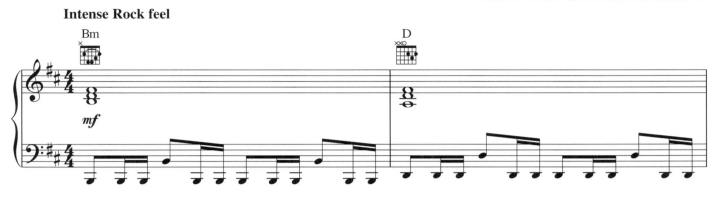

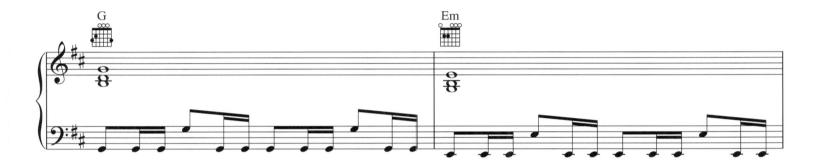

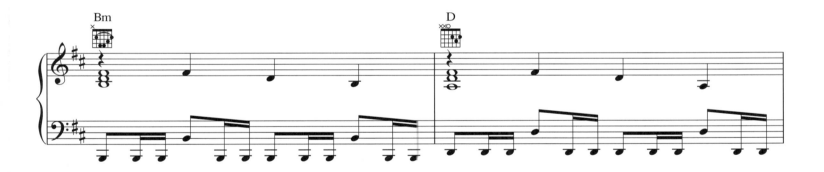

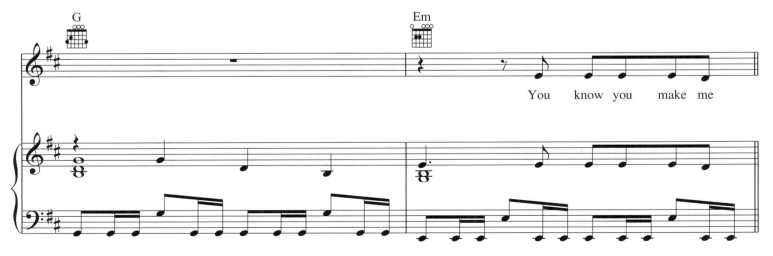

You know you make me

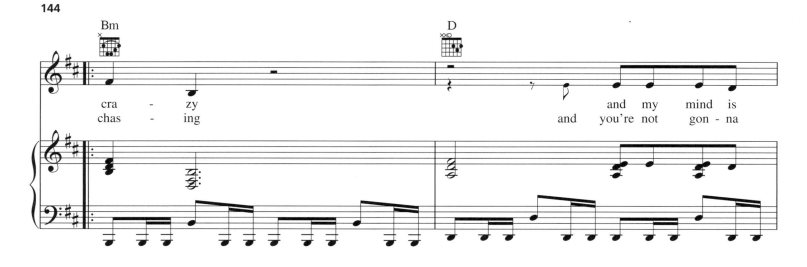

cra - zy
chas - ing

and my mind is
and you're not gon - na

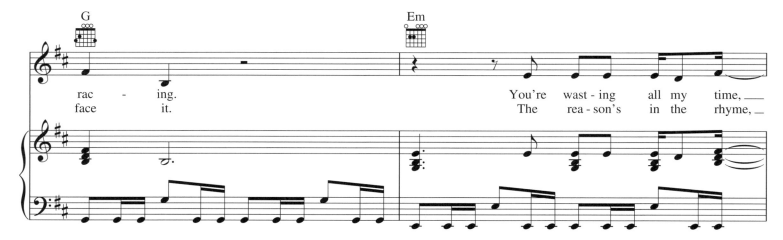

rac - ing.
face it.

You're wast - ing all my time, __
The rea - son's in the rhyme, __

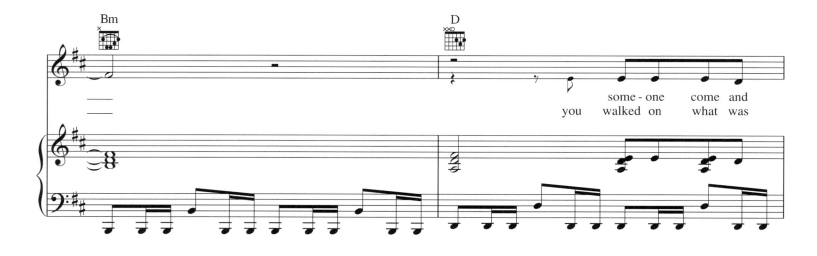

some - one come and
you walked on what was

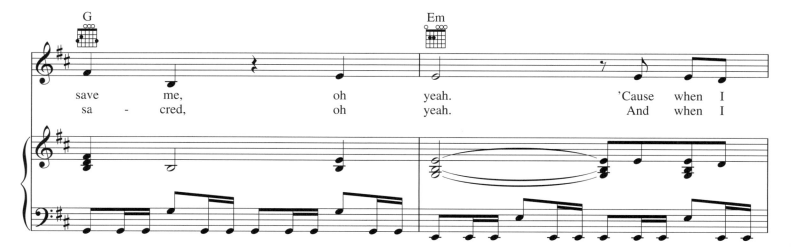

save me,
sa - cred,

oh yeah.
oh yeah.

'Cause when I
And when I

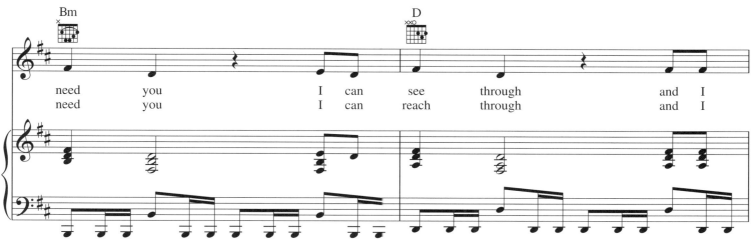

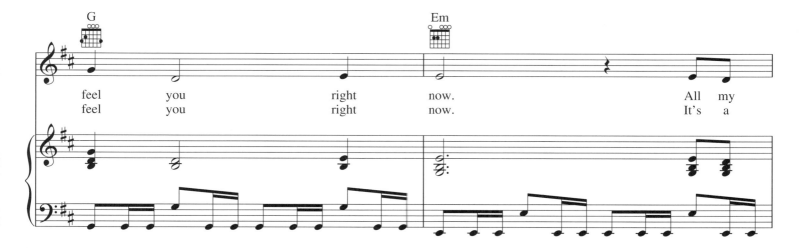

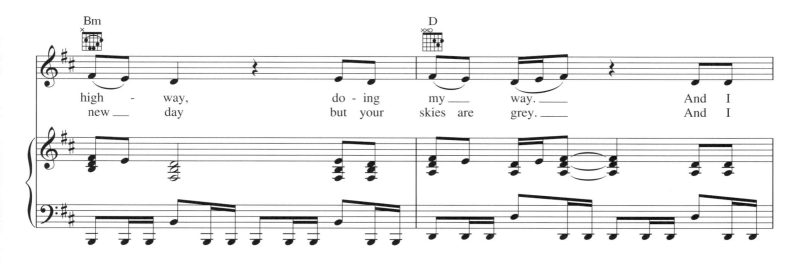

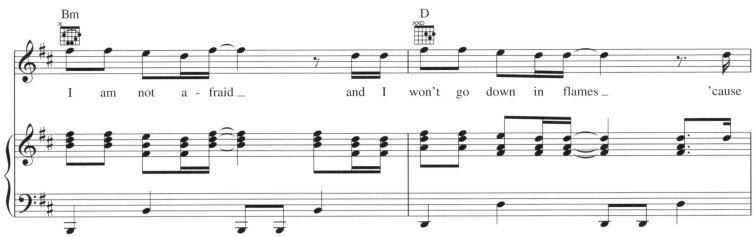

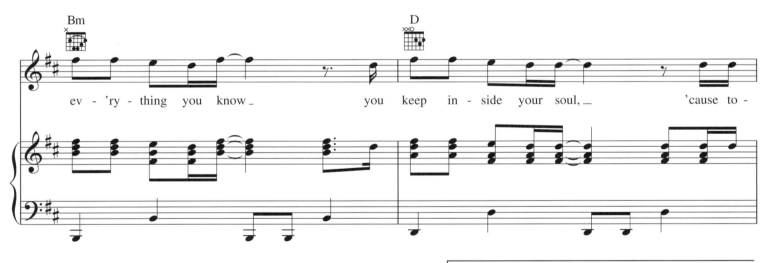

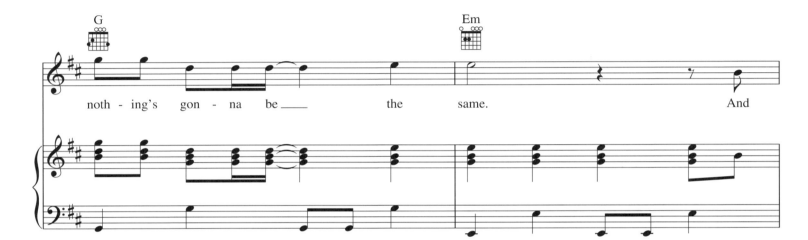

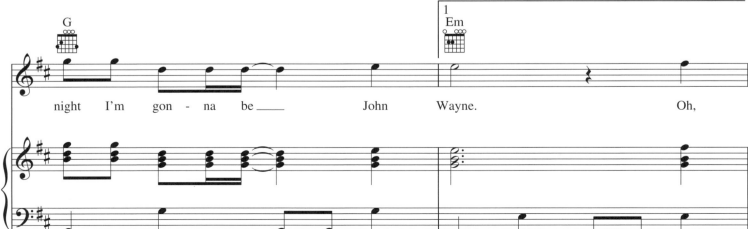

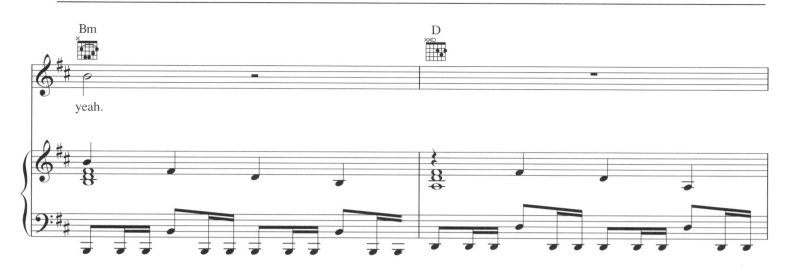

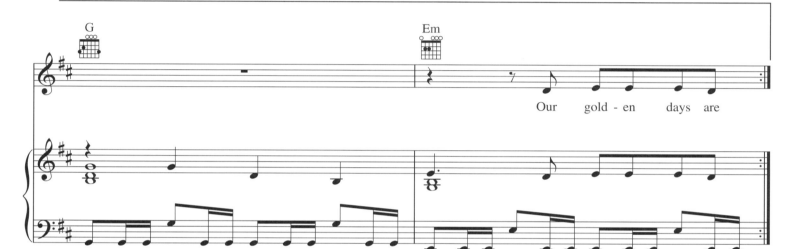

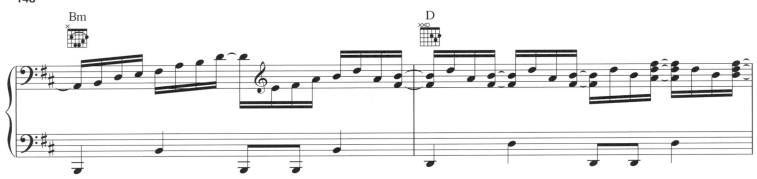

Ev - 'ry - thing you know ___ you keep in - side your soul, ___ 'cause to -

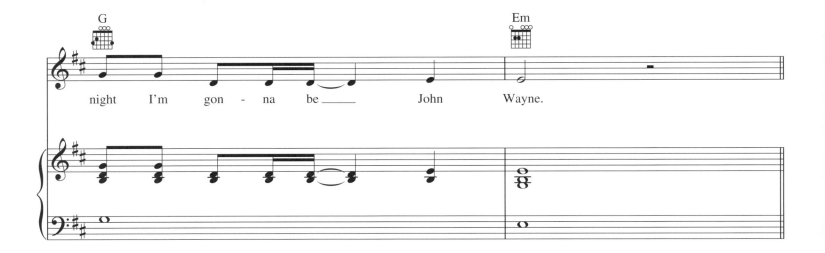

night I'm gon - na be _____ John Wayne.

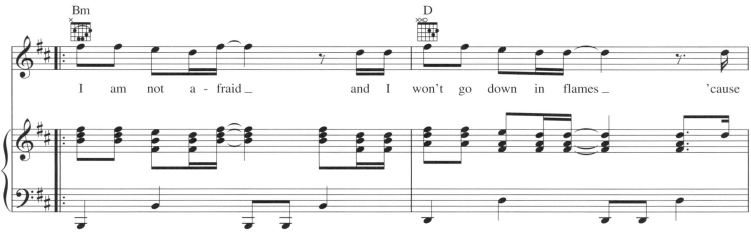

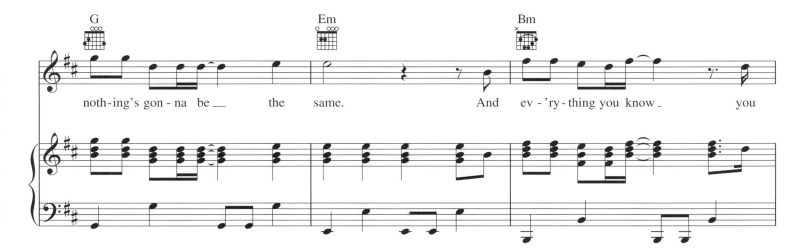

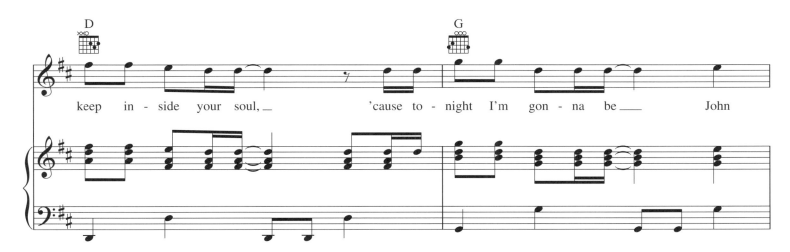

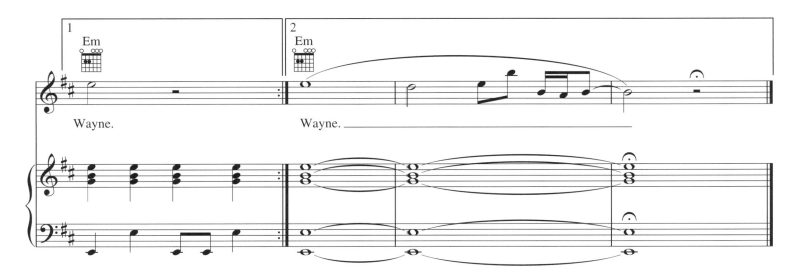

NEW FUTURE WEAPON

Words and Music by BILLY IDOL
and BRIAN TICHY

Driving Rock

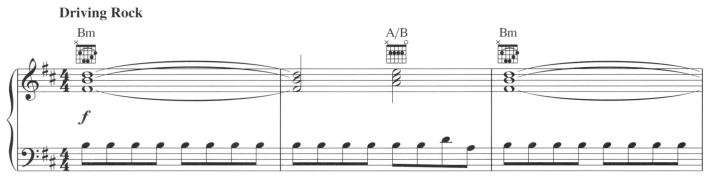

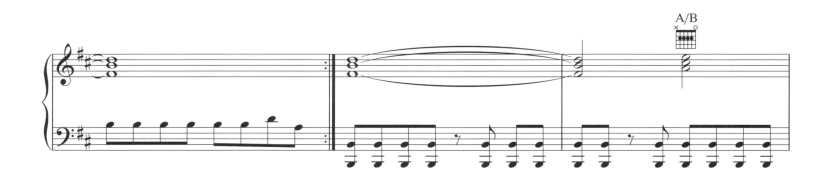

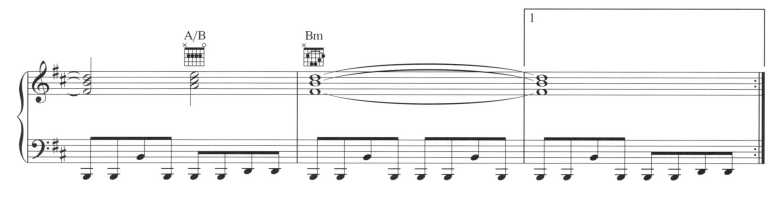

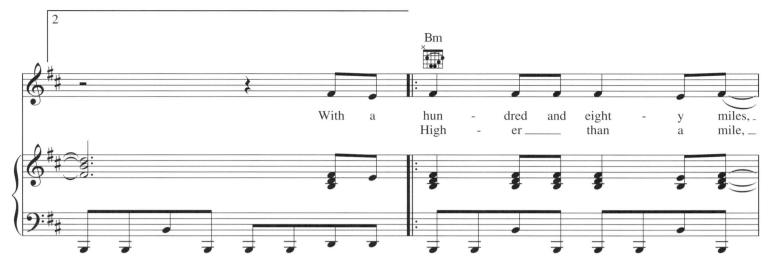

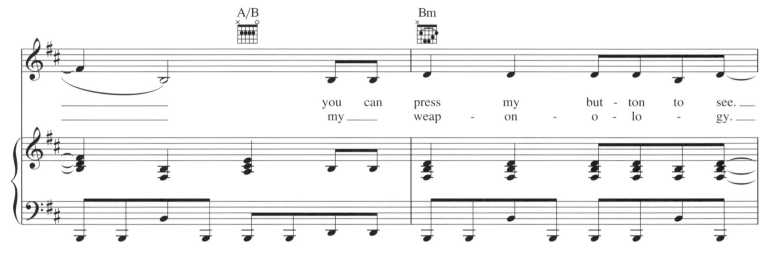

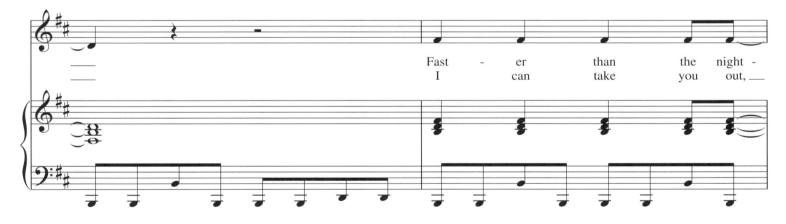

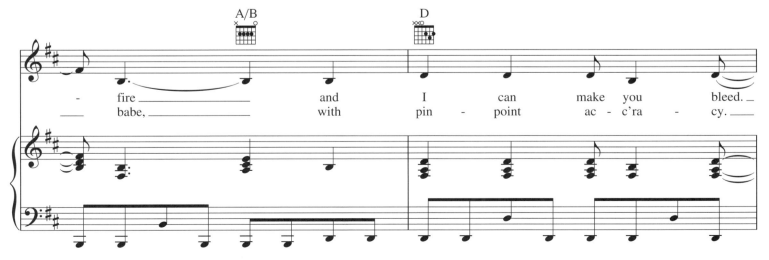

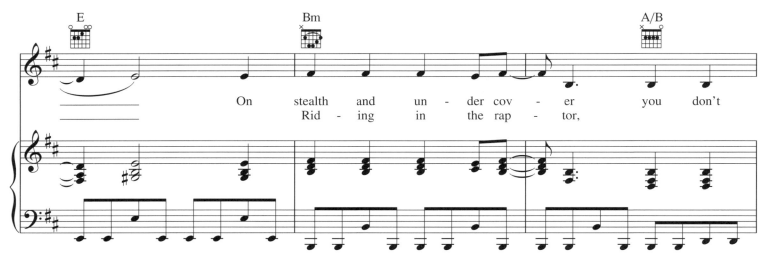

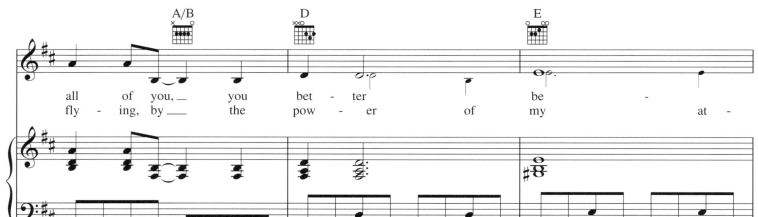

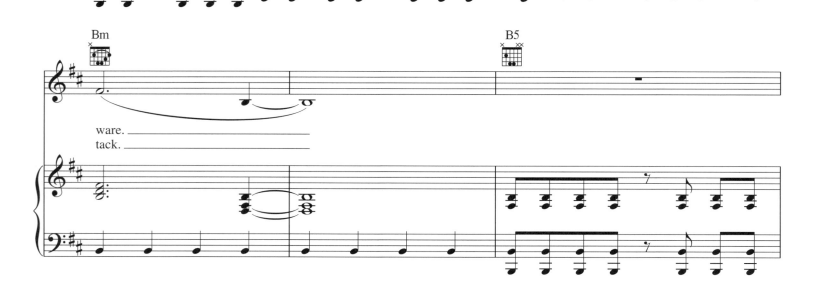

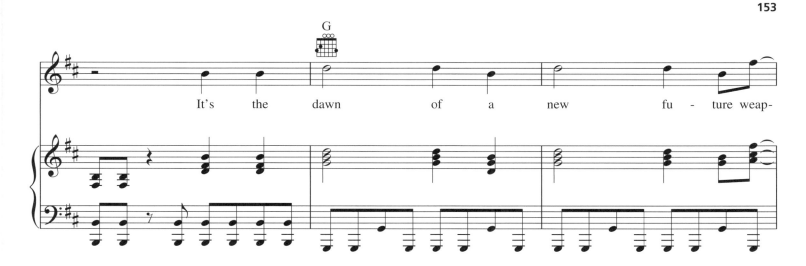

It's the dawn of a new fu - ture weap-

- on, I'm af - ter your soul,

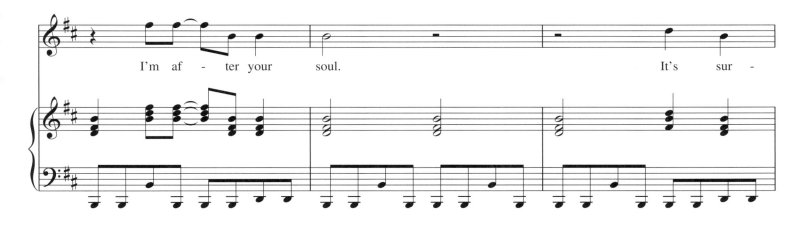

I'm af - ter your soul. It's sur -

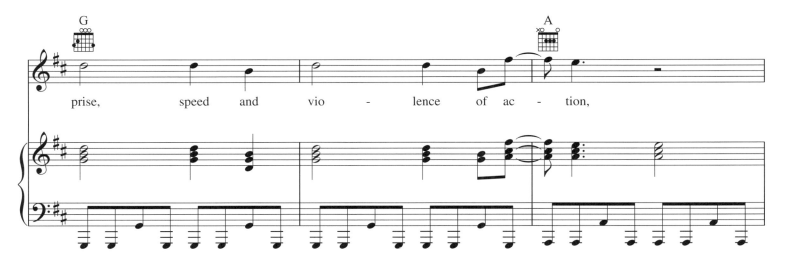

prise, speed and vio - lence of ac - tion,

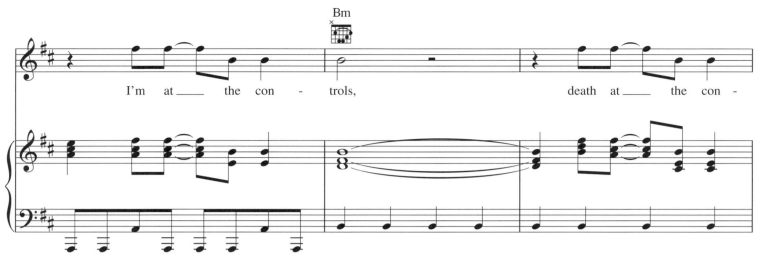

I'm at _____ the con - trols,   death at _____ the con -

trols.

N.C.

Liv-ing in this des-ert,

liv-ing in slime, _ the air you breathe _ is a poi-son-ous fire. _ The

sounds you hear _ de-stroy the tune, _ the sounds you hear _ de-

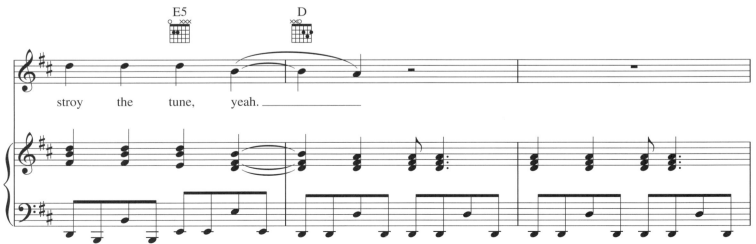

stroy the tune, yeah. _

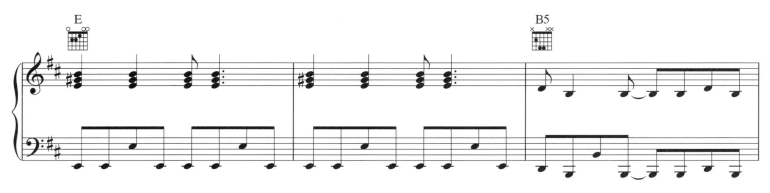

With a hun - dred and eight - y miles _____ you can

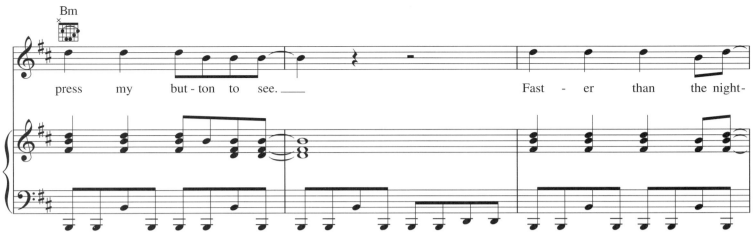

press my but- ton to see. _____ Fast - er than the night-

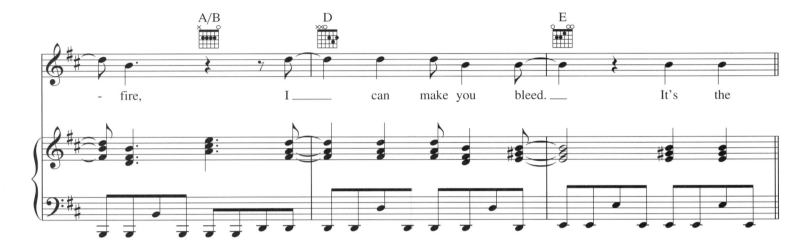

- fire, I _____ can make you bleed. _____ It's the

dawn of a new fu - ture weap - on,

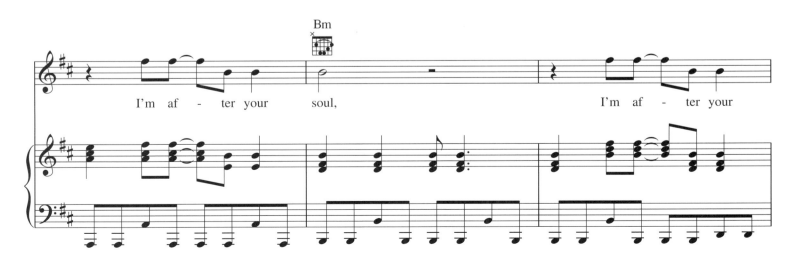

I'm af - ter your soul, I'm af - ter your

soul. It's sur - prise, speed and

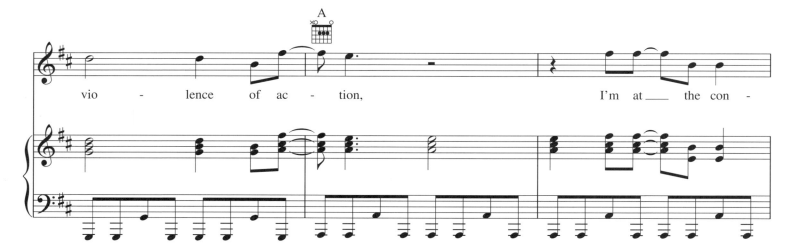

vio - lence of ac - tion, I'm at ___ the con -

trols, death at ___ the con - trols.

It's the

It's the

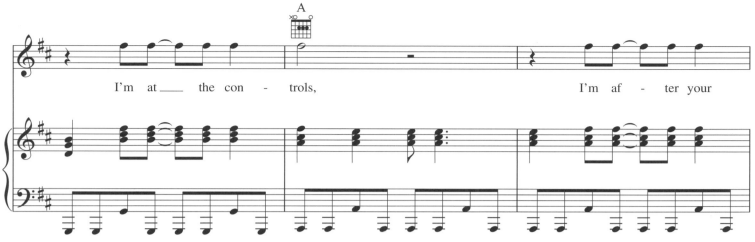

I'm at ____ the con - trols,   I'm af - ter your

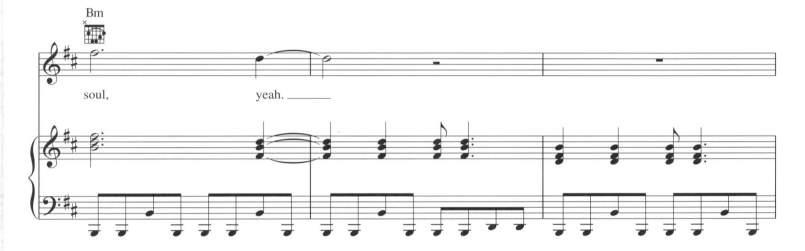

soul,   yeah. ____

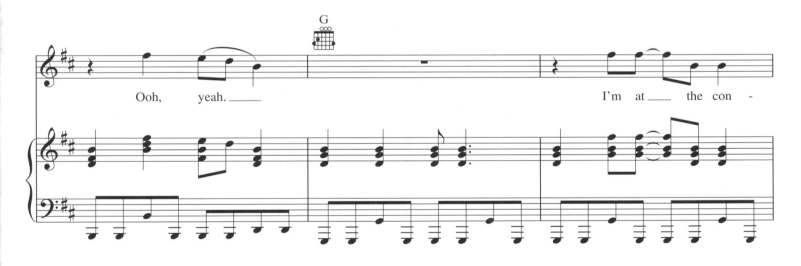

Ooh,   yeah. ____   I'm at ____ the con -

trols,   I'm af - ter your soul.